Human–Computer Interaction Series

SpringerBriefs in Human-Computer Interaction

Series editors

Desney Tan, Microsoft Research, USA
Jean Vanderdonckt, Université catholique de Louvain, Belgium

More information about this series at http://www.springer.com/series/15580

John N.A. Brown · Anton Josef Fercher
Gerhard Leitner

Building an Intuitive Multimodal Interface for a Smart Home

Hunting the SNARK

 Springer

John N.A. Brown
Advertiser User Experience Research Group
Adecco at Google
San Bruno, CA
USA

and

Interactive Systems Group
Alpen-Adria-Universität Klagenfurt
Klagenfurt, Carinthia
Austria

and

Centre Tecnològic de Recerca per a la
 Depedència i la Vida Autònoma
Universitat Politècnica de Catalunya
Catalonia
Spain

and

Signal Processing & Telecommunications
 Group, Department of Electrical,
 Electronic, Telecommunications
 Engineering and Naval Architecture
University of Genoa
Genova
Italy

Anton Josef Fercher
Interactive Systems Group
Alpen-Adria-Universität Klagenfurt
Klagenfurt, Carinthia
Austria

Gerhard Leitner
Interactive Systems Group
Alpen-Adria-Universität Klagenfurt
Klagenfurt, Carinthia
Austria

ISSN 1571-5035
Human–Computer Interaction Series
ISSN 2520-1670   ISSN 2520-1689   (electronic)
SpringerBriefs in Human-Computer Interaction
ISBN 978-3-319-56531-6   ISBN 978-3-319-56532-3   (eBook)
DOI 10.1007/978-3-319-56532-3

Library of Congress Control Number: 2017937117

Printed on acid-free paper

This Springer imprint is published by Springer Nature
The registered company is Springer International Publishing AG
The registered company address is: Gewerbestrasse 11, 6330 Cham, Switzerland

Contents

List of Figures

List of Tables

Abstract

Throughout all of human history, the accurate and precise use of any tool has required an understanding of how that tool was designed to be used. In order to use a tool, we must focus on our purpose while looking through a lens shaped by the perspective of the designer of that tool. Putting it simply, you must know which end of the axe is for holding. In Human–Computer Interaction (HCI) you must understand that a digital stylus is intended for sliding across the monitor, while a mouse is designed to slide across almost any other flat surface. Learning to use a new tool requires learning to think from a new perspective. Usually, increased complexity requires increased learning. We propose an HCI approach that inverts the traditional subservience of perspective, forcing the machine to adapt its input and output requirements to suit the user. Our multimodal interaction is based on a smartphone app that combines GUI, text, gestures and voice commands as a step towards intuitive human communication with a smart home. The design of this app, in turn, is based on theories from psychology, engineering, and linguistics that are decades old. Shown how to perform two tasks, 32 participants were asked to intuit how to control seven other networked and embedded devices through intuitive multimodal interaction based on universal mental models. First attempts were between 28.1% and 90.6% successful. By the third consecutive attempt, successes ranged from 65.6% on one device, to 100% on four others. The process of using old ideas to shape the use of new technology is explained in detail in the following volume showing, in all deference to Jorge Santayana, that those who remember the past are sometimes blessed to repeat it.

Chapter 1
"...A Lesson in Natural History": Introduction to the Smart Home

Abstract Human evolution is intertwined with technology evolution, from wooden tools to computers. In the 1990s Weiser announces ubiquitous computing, and called for an re-imagining of computerized systems, making them "calm". This chapter addresses the historical developments of smart environments in general and smart homes in particular, referring to first attempts considered as smart, e.g. from Leonardo and emphasizing the wrong technology-oriented approach in the field—as shown by the Honeywell kitchen computer. An attempt to change to a more non-technical and HCI-driven approach is shown with the example of the Casa Vecchia project, concluding the chapter.

Keywords Evolution · Smart home · Wise home · Domotics · HCI · History of home automation

The evolution and adaptation of humans is intractably intertwined with the evolution and adaptation of our technology [1]. This was true when our ancestors added wooden handles to stone adzes, and it is true today. Around twenty years ago Mark Weiser warned that Ubiquitous Computing (UC) would require the development of a tremendous change to the way in which we interact with computers and the machines that house them [2]. His prediction of ubiquity has come true and we are surrounded by computerized systems that shape most of our day-to-day interactions with technology [3]. Despite the ubiquity of computers and computerization we have done very little to adapt the proliferating technology to our new way of life [4]. Weiser's proposed solution, "Calm Technology" (CT) describes tools made to suit the natural ways in which humans perceive, process, and respond to the world [5]. He called for a re-imagining of how we interact with computerized systems, so that the entire process could become more suitable to human abilities and limitations [6].

Answering that call, we have demonstrated intuitive interaction with 32 un-familiarized volunteers with a subset of the heterogeneous computerized devices found in the standard home of the 21st Century. Shown how to remotely perform 2 normal day-to-day tasks, our participants went on to intuit how to perform 7 others

© The Author(s) 2017
J.N.A. Brown et al., *Building an Intuitive Multimodal Interface for a Smart Home*,
Human–Computer Interaction Series, DOI 10.1007/978-3-319-56532-3_1

with a smart phone app that allowed two very different types of multimodal interaction; one centering on natural speech and the other centered on familiar gestures.

1.1 Smart Environments

From cockpits and nuclear power plants to the average 21st century home theatre or media center; from virtual reality-augmented surgical theatres to immersive-gameplay arcades; smart environments are no longer restricted to science fiction. In fact, it can be postulated that, given the ubiquitous use of smartphones, their expanding toolset, and the almost universal nature of connectedness, we now carry our smart environments with us. Ubiquitous computing has turned not only our homes and workplaces, but even the most prosaic environment (a train, a car, or a city park) into a node in a network of embedded systems. The average person may not even be aware of the degree to which they are connected. Since the dawn of the internet and the beginnings of incidental connectivity, our proclivity for connectivity and our demand for service have surpassed all predictions. One area in which this proclivity has been a driving force is the domestication of the technology behind smart environments. We will now review the history and state of the art of this subset of smart environments, the Smart Home, before returning to the more general field to conclude our discussion.

1.2 The Smart Home

Research into smart homes has been going on for decades and detailed reviews of the literature have been conducted by Cook and Das [7–9], by Chan et al. [10], and more recently by De Silva, Morikawa and Petra [11]. The focus of these studies is often on Active and Assisted Living (AAL) for the elderly [12] or for people with special needs [13, 14], but the entry threshold for AAL is dropping with the advent of innovative design and technology integration [15]. This is changing the nature of smart environments, especially as technological advances allow display and control to change from single-user to multi-user [16].

Leonardo da Vinci gave us what may be the first documented transcription of technological innovations into normal living space in his folios numbered 16r and 37v, as seen in the collection of codices of the *Institut de France* [17]. It wasn't until the early 20th Century that the modern concept of a home technology entered the public consciousness, largely in the form of comedy in which incredibly-complex, automated, Rube Goldberg-style machines were proposed as a means to "simplify" day-to-day tasks, such as the feeding machine in Charlie Chaplin's "Modern Times" [18]. The advent of practical computer technology in the middle of that century, and the creation of the first mass-produced microchips led to the beginnings of home automation. Simple devices such as remote controls for televisions and garage door openers were quickly accepted internationally [19]. More complex devices generated publicity but not sales. One example is the "Honeywell Kitchen Computer" (H316 pedestal model) offered in the Neiman Marcus consumer catalogue in the United States in 1969 [20]. This machine was advertised as being able to help housewives plan their menus and budgets, but it was roughly three times as expensive as a house and required that the user take a two-week course in order to learn to use the toggle-switch input panel and to read the flashing binary light output.

Both price and demands on the user would have to be lowered before computerized assistive devices could become realistically viable in the home. It is interesting to note that, according to Atkinson, Gordon Bell [Vice President of Engineering at Digital Equipment Corporation (DEC)] wrote a memo describing possible improvements to the "Honeywell Kitchen Computer" that was the inspiration for DEC to enter the field of domotic computing. In fact, in the memo, Bell wrote that, with an improved interface, a home computer could be directed not at the kitchen but for use with entertainment, games and studying [21]. By the end of the century, Smart Home systems were being developed and tested in academic and corporate laboratories around the world [22].

One of the major drivers in the quest to build Smart Home technology is the profit motive of certain groups of developers who show little concern for how the technology will be used or whether it is compatible with other technology. In 2002, Zayas-Cabán proposed a methodology for conducting home assessments in order to implement specialized technological systems that suit the house and the inhabitants [23]. As discussed a decade earlier in the Report of the European Foundation for the Improvement of Living and Working Conditions, the manufacturers of technological devices were putting the cart before the horse: rather than assess the environment and develop technology in response to needs, they were waiting until after technology was developed and deployed before worrying about how suitable it might be [24]. This has led to a vast treasure trove of commercial systems and components and to a dearth of commercial attempts to work with other developers. The void is being filled now, at least on a theoretical level, and many academic and commercial research teams are turning their attention to finding not just models, but actual working systems for the unification of commercially and technologically diverse distributed Smart Home interfaces.

Many of the Smart Home systems developed to date have two unfortunate elements in common with the kitchen computer discussed above: they remain expensive (despite some improvement), and they make high demands on the user. Both of these elements were addressed in the Casa Vecchia project [25].

1.3   Casa Vecchia: Making an "Old House" Smart

Leitner and Fercher developed Casa Vecchia, a Smart Home project that was outstanding when it was started, not only for addressing issues of cost and cognitive load; and not only for setting out to evaluate the viability of deploying Smart Home systems in their community; but mainly because it deals with the oft-ignored guideline suggested by Venkatesh:

> Don't assume that what the technology can do in the household is the same as what the household wants to do with the technology [26].

After a decade of conducting anthropological-style field studies and large-scale longitudinal and cross-sectional surveys in order to determine the technological and social elements affecting technological diffusion in the home, Venkatesh developed an underlying theoretical structure that included a conceptual model of the *cyber-household* [26]. His theory of household-technology interaction is generated from a modified structural-functionalist approach that has sound footings in ethnography but is largely ignored by the technological community.

Leitner and Fercher, like Venkatesh, approach the Smart Home from the points of view of both utilitarian material culture (focusing on tools and tool use) and a socio-psychological approach in which the social dynamics of the household must be paramount. By combining these perspectives, Venkatesh was able to model the use of technology in relation to household structure, and so propose a dynamic and adapting system that would change according to the needs or wants of the occupants of the home. This dynamic, human-focused application of technology is exactly what Leitner and Fercher set out to apply and study, in the hopes of "... finding as many missing pieces of the jigsaw of UX in the context of AAL as possible".

They have done this by combining HCI approaches to the human side of the equation with innovative applications of off-the-shelf technology while standing on the shoulders of those who have gone before them. To use their words:

> The focus of the project is to deploy a customized system into more or less arbitrary homes based on the achievements gained by researchers all over the world [25].

The homes in question are the real houses of real people in the province of Carinthia, Austria. The number fluctuated, but at any given time, there were about 20 active homes involved. The senior citizens living in these homes agreed to the introduction of domotic technology, but with the promise from the researchers that this would be done in a slow and smooth manner. They, their families and their primary caretakers were all involved in an ongoing process of feedback and response as the researchers and the participants co-developed the customized systems that best suit the household. The results of longitudinal surveys will soon be available. In the meantime, though the whole range of results has been yet to be reported, this truly human-focused means of developing a smart environment was instrumental in fostering the theoretical and practical work reported in this brief.

References

1. Brown JNA (2013) It's as Easy as ABC: introducing anthropology-based computing. In: Advances in computational intelligence. Springer, Berlin, pp 1–16
2. Weiser M (1991) The computer for the twenty-first century. Sci Am 265(3):94–104
3. Weiser M, Brown JS (1996) Designing calm technology. PowerGrid J 1(1):75–85
4. Weiser M, Brown JS (1997) The coming age of calm technology. In: Denning PJ, Metcalfe RM (eds) Beyond calculation: the next fifty years of computing. Copernicus, New York, pp 75–85
5. Weiser M (1993) Some computer science issues in ubiquitous computing. Commun ACM 36 (7):75–84
6. Weiser M (1994) The world is not a desktop. Interactions 1(1):7–8
7. Cook DJ (2012) How smart is your home? Science 335(6076):1579–1581
8. Cook DJ, Das SK (2012) Pervasive computing at scale: transforming the state of the art. Pervasive Mob Comput 8(1):22–35
9. Cook DJ, Das SK (2007) How smart are our environments? An updated look at the state of the art. Pervasive Mob Comput 3(2):53–73
10. Chan M, Estève D, Escriba C, Campo E (2008) A review of smart homes—present state and future challenges. Comput Methods Programs Biomed 9(I):55–81
11. De Silva LC, Morikawa C, Petra IM (2012) State of the art of smart homes. Eng Appl Artif Intell 25(7):1313–1321
12. Díaz Boladeras M, Casacuberta Bagó J, Nuño Bermudez N, Berbegal Mirabent J, Berbegal Mirabent N (2011) Evaluación con usuarios finales durante el desarrollo de dos sistemas interactivos orientados a personas mayores. In: Proc. XI Congreso Internacional de Interacción Persona-Ordenador 2010, València, pp 411–420
13. Brandt ÅÅ, Samuelsson K, Tööytääri O, Salminen AL (2011) Activity and participation, quality of life and user satisfaction outcomes of environmental control systems and smart home technology: a systematic review. Disabil Rehabil Assistive Technol 6(3):189
14. Myers BA (1998) A brief history of human-computer interaction technology. Interactions 5 (2):44–54
15. Leitner G, Fercher A (2010) AAL 4 ALL A matter of user experience. In: Aging friendly technology for health and independence. Springer, Berlin, pp 195–202
16. Felfernig A, Mandl M, Tiihonen J, Schubert M, Leitner G (2010) Personalized user interfaces for product configuration. In: Proceedings of the 15th international conference on intelligent user interfaces, pp 317–320
17. Leonardo (1448) Manuscript B, Folios 16r and 37v in the collection of codices of the Institut de France. Bibliothèque de l'Institut de France, Paris
18. Modern Times (1936) Dir. Charles Chaplin. Perf. Chaplin and Paulette Goddard. United Artists
19. Van Dantzich M, Robbins D, Horvitz E, Czerwinski M (2002). Scope: providing awareness of multiple notifications at a glance. In: Proceedings of the working conference on advanced visual interfaces, ACM, pp 267–281
20. Atkinson P (2010) The curious case of the kitchen computer: products and non-products in design history. J Des Hist 23(2):163–179
21. Bell GA (1969) Congeries on the computer-in-the-home market, internal memorandum of digital equipment corporation dated 11 December 1969. Accession no. 102630372, archives of the computer history museum
22. Zayas-Cabán T (2002) Introducing information technology into the home: conducting a home assessment. In: Proceedings of the AMIA symposium. American Medical Informatics Association, p 924

23. Paoli P, Litske H (1992) First European survey on the work environment 1991–1992. European Foundation for the Improvement of Living and Working Conditions, Dublin
24. Leitner G, Fercher A, Felfernig A, Hitz M (2012) Reducing the entry threshold of AAL systems: preliminary results from casa vecchia. In: Miesenberger K, Karshmer A, Penaz P, Zagler W (eds) Computers helping people with special needs lecture notes in computer science, vol 7382, 1st edn. Springer, Heidelberg, pp 709–715
25. Leitner G, Fercher AJ (2011) Potenziale und Herausforderungen von AAL im ländlichen Raum. In: Proceedings of Ambient assisted living 2011. Berlin, Germany
26. Venkatesh A (1996) Computers and other interactive technologies for the home. Commun ACM 39(12):47–54

Chapter 2
"...If I Had but the Time and You Had but the Brain...": Computer-Centered Computing

Abstract Evolution of the smart home has, to a large extent, been driven by technological developments, frequently neglecting actual human needs and habits. To realize the vision of the Wise Home, a shift to a more human-centered approach is needed. In order to move to a more natural interaction, we must first accept that current interaction paradigms are unnatural. In nature, human communication is not based on a single modality, such as speech or gesture alone, but combines them as two separate but overlapping streams of communication.

Keywords Smart home · HCI · Wise home · Output modalities · Gesture-based interaction · Speech-based interaction · Sound-based interaction · Natural communication

In January, 2011, the US National Science Foundation gathered a group of 72 international researchers in Seattle to discuss the multidisciplinary problems involved in the future of networking smart tools. The discussion is summarized by Cook and Das [1]. The workshop and resultant paper focus on scalability as the key issue for the future. They broke down their concerns into eight subfields, only one of which directly focused on the human factors in HCI.

This focus on the machines rather than the people who should use them is a weakness in past and current trends in pervasive computing, despite the relatively long history of applying the perspectives of cultural anthropology and sociology to the adoption of cyber technology [2, 3]. It is a shame to think that this will continue into the future, but consider the opening sentence of the summary paper mentioned above:

> The remarkable recent growth in computing power, sensors and embedded devices, smart phones, wireless communications and networking combined with the power of data mining techniques and emerging support for cloud computing and social networks has enabled researchers and practitioners to create a wide variety of pervasive computing systems that reason intelligently, act autonomously, and respond to the needs of the users in a context- and situation-aware manner [1].

The idea that intelligent agents should be making hidden decisions on behalf of humans is totally against the idea of Ubiquitous Computing (UC) mitigated with

© The Author(s) 2017
J.N.A. Brown et al., *Building an Intuitive Multimodal Interface for a Smart Home*, Human–Computer Interaction Series, DOI 10.1007/978-3-319-56532-3_2

Calm Technology (CT) as envisaged by Weiser. Despite that, and despite Weiser's direct warning, as cited above, researchers have continued in their attempts to generate intelligent agents intended to make decisions so that humans don't have to. Consider Diane J. Cook's monograph in the March 2012 issue of Science [4], wherein she expresses an indiscriminate overlap between pervasive computing, ubiquitous computing and ambient intelligence, positing a home or work environment that is entirely under the control of intelligent agents. This is a far cry from the "gentle enhancement" of the natural environment with "self-effacing" interfaces that would "leave you feeling as though you did it yourself" posited by Weiser [5]. In fact, the idea of smart environments based around intelligent agents seems to be the inverse of Weiser's idea of "Machines that fit the human environment instead of forcing humans to enter theirs" [6].

If it is accepted that using computers causes stress when the user feels that they are not in control, as per Riedl et al. [7], then it is a natural extension to assume that such stress would be an even greater threat in an immersive, computer-centered environment such as a smart home. Interviews and focus group sessions have shown that users prefer a centralized remote control to enable immediate interaction with a number of devices installed in a household [8]. While the concept of a control panel proved popular, as an interface [9], it is an artifact from what Weiser called the *Mainframe Era* of computing [5]. However, it may not be good to concentrate interaction with a smart environment into a single device for at least two reasons. First, if the central device does not function appropriately, the function of the whole system is affected. Second, in a conventional home, interfaces are distributed and used in combination depending on the task at hand. Given that technology were to develop appropriately, it might be a better alternative to have a system based on more or less equally powerful components distributed throughout the environment. This is what Norman called the appliances based approach, and it conforms to the current "apps" philosophy on smartphones and tablets, within which each component has a clearly defined and delimited function and responsibility.

Some researchers, such as Chan et al. [10], foresee the coming of either wearable or implantable systems to complement domotic control with the provision of biomedical monitoring sensors. While "apps" are state-of-the-art, it will be some time before these features can become ubiquitous. Chan et al. go on to stress that since smart homes promise to improve comfort, leisure and safety the interaction should be as natural as possible. If their proposed method of improvement is still developing technologically, our proposed method is built upon applying currently available technology in a novel manner.

2.1   Human-Computer Interaction

Early human-computer interaction was a multi-stage process, requiring that several specialists work on a single project. Those requiring computer assistance would consult these specialists, whose skill was the ability to communicate with the machine. Since the machine, in those days, was essentially a series of on/off switches, all of the input mechanisms provided serial information; hundreds, thousands, even millions of noughts and ones.

The first area of specialization was the translation of the question into problems that could be presented to the computer. A question would have to be expressed as a series of logic problems, the sort that could be answered "yes" or "no". The series of questions framed by the logicians had then to be translated into "machine language" by a group of translators, and then passed on to experts who created tapes or punch-cards. These were then passed on to the technicians who actually worked with the machine. According to one account:

> This seems vastly more complex than the computer systems that we use now, but the only real difference is that most of the specialized steps in the process of human-computer interaction are now performed by the computer, rather than by the human [11].

To paraphrase Myers [12]; the change that allowed HCI to move from a field for experts to a field for common use was the realization that, through the addition of processing power, the machine could assume most of the expert roles. This was a great breakthrough in the proliferation of computers into day-to-day life. Unfortunately, as shown from the continued use of obsolete 400 codes for flagging errors (like the common "Error 404"), it gave the world a working model of computer-centered interaction that we have still not overcome. To evolve past computer-centered computing, one necessary step will be to stop our *Cross-Generational Habit* of designing interaction in accordance with obsolete technological standards like typewriters or TV screens [13]. In its place we should establish new human-centered standards based on a better understanding of the natural workings of our brains and on simple, observable facts. One example that is pertinent to HCI is the observable fact that human communication naturally involves complementing words with gestures.

2.2   A Gesture of Goodwill

> In gestures we are able to see the imagistic form of the speaker's sentences. This imagistic form is not usually meant for public view, and the speaker him- or herself may be unaware of it... [14]

As we have already said, all natural human interaction is multimodal; we constrain ourselves to a single modality only when required. When in a diving environment, scuba gear enables us to function without having to learn to breathe underwater, but formal communication is reduced to a single modality and becomes dependent on the use of strictly-defined and well-practiced gestures. When in a digital environment, the GUI interface enables us to function without having to learn machine language, but formal communication is reduced to a single modality and becomes dependent on the use of strictly defined and severely truncated words which have been removed from their usual ontological, cultural and environmental context.

Hurtienne et al. produced what they claim is "the first study looking into primary metaphors for gesture interaction in inclusive design" [15]. Their paper proposes the construction of physical gestures, based on the aggregate of twelve of what they called primary metaphors from other published studies. This list is quoted directly from theirs:

(1) Important is central, unimportant is peripheral.
(2) The future is in front, the past is behind.
(3) Progress is forward movement, undoing progress is backward movement.
(4) Similar is near, different is far.
(5) Familiar is near, unfamiliar is far.
(6) Considered is near, not considered is far.
(7) Good is near, bad is far.
(8) Good is up, bad is down.
(9) More is up, less is down.
(10) Happy is up, sad is down.
(11) Virtue is up, depravity is down.
(12) Power is up, powerless is down.

In each case, the authors quote spoken phrases that were used to support the metaphor in the original paper. At best these examples are facile, as in the pair "I feel close to him. He distances himself" used to illustrate number 5, which is easily countered with the common phrase "stranger in a strange land". At worst, the chosen phrase does not mean what the authors seem to think. Consider the phrases used to support metaphor number 7: "Here is something interesting. There comes the difficulty." "Here" and there" are interchangeable in the first phrase, and the second phrase would only be correct English if "there" were replaced by "here". This linguistic confusion is unfortunate, but it does not lessen the problem of trying to base a universal gesture on a non-representational subset of world languages. It is possible to generate lexicons of language- or culture-based gestures, as we have seen in the work discussed above. It is also possible that there will be some overlap between these gestures and any new lexicon of truly universal ones. Such an overlap, however, may be much smaller than one would initially anticipate.

If one were to pursue the idea of universal gestures, which is not the intent of this work, it might be better to turn away from simplified contrasting pairs like "up" and "down". Consider that up and down can both mean, "at hand", "within easy reach", "within difficult reach", "out of reach" and "far beyond reach".

High or low, "out of reach" has a meaning that is universal. It is different from "within reach", and both are different from "in-hand" and "unreachable", but none of them are opposites. Neither are "hot and cold". "Too hot" and "too cold" can both be mapped as cognitive vectors away from a concept of comfort. Maybe we can agree that they are both going through the realm of "discomfort", towards a concept of "environmentally fatal", but these would clearly all be best conceptualized as concentric spheres rather than 1-dimensional lines.

Leaving aside these logical flaws, Hurtienne et al. claim that their metaphors have not been influenced by technology. This claim is refuted in their examples and through simple inductive reasoning. To wit: the experimenters and participants have all been influenced by underlying mental models in their most basic technological tools, such as the Cartesian increase in value when a switch is pushed either to the right or upward, and the decrease when the same switch moves in the opposite direction. Since these underlying concepts are applied globally, it would seem obvious to save time and trouble by simply using them as the basis of gestural interaction. Our attempt to do so, is described in Chap. 5.

The technology that supports gesture detection has greatly dropped in price and increased in popularity with the advent of gesture-based video game interfaces. This started with actively-broadcasting sensors in handheld gameplay controllers and active motion detectors in stationary consoles. Further improvements in the availability of gestural interaction have come from the development of smartphone applications that take advantage of the increasing presence and improved performance of accelerometers, magnetometers and gyroscopes. Despite the usability afforded by the increasing ubiquity of smartphones, empty-handed interaction is still a goal. Cohn et al. proposed a means for using the electromagnetic field generated by normal in-home wiring to detect the location, orientation, and hand and arm movements of participants in their own homes [16]. Refinements to their method, *Humantenna*, were presented the following year, with results suggesting multi-finger gesture recognition [17]. In both cases, though, the participants had to wear a backpack full of equipment. This volume is our response; a proposal for smartphone-based gestures and empty-handed interaction.

We do not want to create a gestural recognition system based on the false paradigm of single modality interaction. Instead, our gestures will amplify spoken word interaction, observing the same phonological synchronicity rules that have been observed when gestures consciously or unconsciously accompany speech in normal interaction [18]. Rather than succumb to the common behavior of designating a black box to encapsulate technological issues that have not yet been resolved but do seem to be imminently soluble, we have turned to an old triple-redundancy protocol that was used a generation ago on satellite control systems [19]. Our attempt, the S.N.A.R.K., is mentioned again below and discussed in detail in Chap. 4.

2.3   Speech and Sound

The control of networked and embedded systems through the use of automatic speech recognition has long been a feature of science fiction and fantasy interfaces, but the idea of implementing the technology in the real world predates the modern computer era, as reflected in the first volume of Natural Communication with Computers, from Woods et al. 1974 [20]. Even with the development of superior technology, attempts to translate the idea into real life have met only modest success, as is reflected in the title of a 2011 conference presentation by Oulasvirta et al., "Communication failures in the speech-based control of smart home systems" [21].

In 2008, Fleury et al. presented a study of speech and sound detection and classification (n = 13) that took place in the Health Smart Home in Grenoble, France [22]. The study is based on the use of 8 ceiling-mounted, omnidirectional microphones that are always turned on. Participants provided data in 3 ways. First they were asked to "make a little scenario" that involved closing a door, making a noise with a cup and spoon, dropping a box on the floor, and screaming the common French exclamation of pain "Aie". This was repeated two more times. Next, each participant had to read 10 "normal" sentences and 20 "distress sentences". Finally, the participant read a conversation into a telephone. Random selections from these separate noises and phrases were then chosen for testing the system. The authors report that the sound recognition results conform to results from laboratory conditions. Speech recognition results were "too low", with 52.38% of the noises made with cup and spoon, and 21.74% of the screams of pain and 62.92% of the distress speech recognized as normal speech. The authors propose that one of the difficulties in speech recognition is that each participant pronounced each phrase differently each time they repeated it. Further weaknesses identified by the authors include background noise, the freedom of the participants to work at their own pace, and the uncontrolled orientation of the speaker vis-a-vis the mounted microphones. Fleury et al. sum up these weaknesses very well: "Thus our conditions are the worst possible, far from the laboratory conditions (no noise and the microphone just behind the subject)" [21]. These weaknesses were used as guidelines for developing our own testing.

In 2009, Hamill et al. also used ceiling-mounted microphones in their proposal of an automated speech recognition interface for use in emergencies [23]. They compared results with a single microphone to an array, in both noisy and quiet conditions (n = 9), and they tested a yes/no response dialog with four participants. Their array performed with 49.9% accuracy, and the single microphone with 29%. Recognition of the words "yes" and "no" was 93% accurate over their 3 scenarios, even though overall word recognition had an error rate of 21%. The researchers suggest that the "reason for this was because the system confirmed the user's selection before taking an action." The authors also report that background noises interfered with the performance of their microphone(s) and that speech recognition was greatly improved by limiting the user's speech to two words. Again, we have been inspired in the design of our experimental protocol, to try and face the specific problems described herein. We were also influenced by another aspect of this study. In the discussion of future work, Hamill et al. mention that, in order to improve the robustness of their automated dialog system, they are developing a speech corpus recorded by an older adult speaking Canadian English. We went on to do the same.

In 2010, Chandak and Dharaskar reported an attempt to implement speech-based controls for a context-sensitive, content-specific Smart Home architecture based on natural language processing [24]. The key to their system was the ability of the user to customize the specific language or languages to be used for input. The paper itself seems incomplete, presenting none of the results promised in the introduction. In fact, no evidence is provided to indicate that the system was implemented at all.

That said, the premise of customizing input language on a dynamic, user-by-user basis informed our theoretical development and the implementation discussed in Chap. 5.

Two teams in France, GETALP in Grenoble and AFIRM in La Tronche, undertook an attempt to design a real-time smart home distress-detection system based on audio technology [25]. They started by testing speech-based detection of distress using a scenario based on a prepared corpus of phrases (n = 10) and reported an overall error rate of 15.6%. For their second experiment, four participants uttered prepared "distress sentences" while a radio news program played in the background. Distress went undetected 27% of the time. In 2010, the same research teams attempted to apply their more advanced sound and speech analysis system (AuditHIS) to the recognition of Activities of Daily Living (ADL) [26]. They attempted to validate their stress-related keyword detection and their algorithm for suppressing background noise while using AuditHIS (and installed sensors) to identify 7 ADLs. They again conducted their experiments in the Habitat Intelligent pour la Santé (HIS) Smart Home, in Grenoble, a site that they describe as "a hostile environment for information acquisition similar to the one that can be encountered in [a] real home". Specifically, they note that uncontrolled noises outside and around the flat reduced their average signal to noise ratio to 12 dB, from the 27 dB measured in their laboratory setting. These normal, uncontrolled, noisy conditions inspired us to address the same issue in both a preparatory study and our final experiment.

As part of France's new Sweet-Home project, Lecouteux, Vacher and Portet compared 7 sources of Automatic Speech Recognition (ASR) [27]. Twenty-one participants recorded pre-determined phrases. Each acoustic model was trained on "about 80 h of annotated speech". In the end, they report that the array of seven microphones improved ASR accuracy and that Beamforming (as in their previous experiments) dropped the Word Error Rate (WER) from their baseline of 18.3% to 16.8%. They found that a Driven Decoding Algorithm (DDA) had only a 11.4% WER and provided slightly better results than the SNR-based ROVER system. Since the computational cost of the DDA is significantly less, and since the DDA would allow for the inclusion of a priori knowledge parameters which would significantly improve the results.

In 2011, Gordon, Passoneau and Epstein presented FORRSooth, a multi-threaded semi-synchronous architecture for spoken dialog systems as an improvement over CheckItOut, their previous pipeline-style architecture [28]. They reported on a pilot study suggesting that helping agents are helpful even when their speech recognition is not perfectly implemented. They addressed the important problem that most ASRs do not allow people to speak naturally during interaction. They suggest that a spoken dialog system (SDS) "should robustly accommodate noisy ASR, and should degrade gracefully as recognition errors increase." This would allow "more nuanced grounding behavior from an SDS" and "help a system understand its user better." These ideas supported our intent to create a dialog system that would help both the software and the user to understand each other better. This nuanced system is described in Chap. 5.

A different kind of sound-based output signal is reported by Bakker et al. [29]. They propose CawClock, an interactive system designed to allow a schoolteacher to set peripheral audio and visual cues by placing tokens depicting distinct animals and colors on the face of an analog clock. These placements cause sections of the clock's face to match the color of that particular token. So long as the minute hand is within the colored area, a background noise that corresponds to the animal is generated by the clock. The volume does not change but the number of animals making the sound increases as time passes, providing subtle cues that time is passing and that the end of the particular timeframe is approaching. Two prototypes were developed. An analog model was provided to the teacher in one classroom for 2 weeks. A mouse-enabled digital version was provided to another. As a reflection of the exploratory nature of the study, the teachers were taught how to use the device but asked to find their own uses for it. Two researchers then attended a 30–45 min classroom session during the second week, taking notes and recording the class on video. The teachers were interviewed singly and together at the end of the second week. Both teachers agreed that the sounds gave themselves and the children signs of passing time during periods of assigned work in the classroom. Both teachers also agreed that they had not noticed the increase in the number of animals over time. Interestingly, and in line with the fundamental understanding of peripheral perception, the ending of a marked period was reportedly more distinct when the background noise changed from one animal to another rather than when it simply ended.

Two unsolved questions in the realm of sound and speech detection have been whether or not to have constant sound detection and whether or not to have a live processor. This would mean a constant drain of both electrical power and processing power. Problems regarding processing power and the extension of battery life are easier to deal with quantitatively. The problems of accurately distinguishing sounds and recognizing speech are generally labeled "not insignificant" and replaced with a black box in flow charts and designs. As with our approach to resolving black box issues in gestural interaction, we have used an old triple-redundancy protocol as the basis of our S.N.A.R.K., a means of facilitating the accurate detection of user intent as communicated through natural means. This is discussed in detail in Chap. 5.

References

1. Cook DJ, Das SK (2012) Pervasive computing at scale: transforming the state of the art. Pervasive Mob Comput 8(1):22–35
2. Escobar A, Hess D, Licha I, Sibley W, Strathern M, Sutz J (1994) Welcome to cyberia: notes on the anthropology of cyberculture [and comments and reply]. Curr Anthropol 35(3): 211–231
3. Zayas-Cabán T (2002) Introducing information technology into the home: conducting a home assessment. In: Proceedings of the AMIA symposium. American Medical Informatics Association, p 924

4. Cook DJ (2012) How smart is your home? Science 335(6076):1579–1581
5. Weiser M (1993) Hot topics-ubiquitous computing. Computer 26(10):71–72
6. Weiser M (1991) The computer for the twenty-first century. Sci Am 265(3):94–104
7. Riedl R, Kindermann H, Auinger A, Javor A (2012) Technostress from a neurobiological perspective. Bus Inf Syst Eng 4(2):61–69
8. Lee S, Koubek RJ (2010) Understanding user preferences based on usability and aesthetics before and after actual use. Interact Comput 22(6):530–543
9. Rauterberg M (1996) Quantitative test metrics to measure the quality of user interfaces. In: Proceedings of 4th European conferences on software testing analysis & review EuroSTAR96, Amsterdam
10. Chan M, Estève D, Escriba C, Campo E (2008) A review of smart homes—present state and future challenges. Computer Methods Programs Biomed 9(I)::55–81
11. Brown JNA (2004) A New input device: comparison to three commercially available mouses. Doctoral dissertation, University of New Brunswick
12. Myers BA (1998) A brief history of human-computer interaction technology. Interactions 5 (2):44–54
13. Brown JNA "Expert talk for time machine session: designing calm technology "… as refreshing as taking a walk in the woods"," 2012 IEEE international conference on Multimedia and Expo, vol 1, pp 423
14. McNeill D (1992) Hand and mind: what gestures reveal about thought. University of Chicago Press, Chicago
15. Hurtienne J, Stößel C, Sturm C, Maus A, Rötting M, Langdon P, Clarkson J (2010) Physical gestures for abstract concepts: inclusive design with primary metaphors. Interact Comput 22 (6):475–484
16. Cohn G, Morris D, Patel SN, Tan DS (2011) Your noise is my command: sensing gestures using the body as an antenna. In: Proceedings of the 2011 annual conference on Human factors in computing systems, vol 1. ACM, pp 791–800
17. Cohn G, Morris D, Patel SN, Tan DS (2012) Humantenna: using the body as an antenna for real-time whole-body interaction. In: Proceedings of the 2011 annual conference on human factors in computing systems
18. McEvoy SP, Stevenson MR, Woodward M (2007) The prevalence of, and factors associated with, serious crashes involving a distracting activity. Accid Anal Prev 39(3):475–482
19. Kaschmitter JL, Shaeffer DL, Colella NJ, McKnett CL, Coakley PG (1991) Operation of commercial R3000 processors in the Low Earth Orbit (LEO) space environment. IEEE Transactions on Nucl Sci 38(6):1415–1420
20. Woods WA, Bates MA, Bruce BC, Colarusso JJ, Cook CC (1974) Natural communication with computers. Speech understanding research at BBN (No. BBN-2976, vol I). Bolt Beranek and Newman Inc. Cambridge, Massachusetts
21. Oulasvirta A et al. (2007). Communication failures in the speech-based control of smart home systems. 3rd IET international conference on Intelligent Environments (IE 07), pp 135–143
22. Fleury A, Noury N, Vacher M, Glasson H, Seri JF (2008) Sound and speech detection and classification in a health smart home. Engineering in Medicine and Biology Society, 2008. EMBS 2008. 30th annual international conference of the IEEE, pp 4644–4647
23. Hamill M, Young V, Boger J, Mihailidis A (2009) Development of an automated speech recognition interface for personal emergency response systems. J Neuroengineering Rehabil 6:26
24. Chandak MB, Dharaskar R (2010) Natural language processing based context sensitive, content specific architecture & its speech based implementation for smart home applications. Int J Smart Home 4(2):1–9
25. Vacher M, Istrate D, Portet F, Joubert T, Chevalier T, Smidtas S, Meillon B, Lecouteux B, Sehili M, Chahuara P, Méniard S (2011) The sweet-home project: audio technology in smart homes to improve well-being and reliance. In: 33rd annual international IEEE EMBS conference, Boston, Massachusetts, USA

26. Fleury A, Vacher M, Noury N (2010) SVM-based multimodal classification of activities of daily living in health smart homes: sensors, algorithms, and first experimental results. IEEE Trans Inf Technol Biomed 14(2):274–283
27. Lecouteux B, Vacher M, Portet F (2011) Distant speech recognition in a smart home: comparison of several multisource ASRs in realistic conditions. In: Interspeech 2011 Florence pp 2273–2276
28. Gordon JB, Passonneau RJ, Epstein SL (2011) Helping agents help their users despite imperfect speech recognition. AAAI symposium help me help you: bridging the gaps in human-agent collaboration
29. Bakker S, van den Hoven E, Eggen B, Overbeeke K (2012) Exploring peripheral interaction design for primary school teachers. In: Proceedings of the sixth international conference on tangible, embedded and embodied interaction, pp 245–252

Chapter 3
"Just the Place for a Snark!": An Introduction to Calm Technology

Abstract What is the difference between how information is presented in nature and on computers? According to Professor Mark Weiser, the core difference is the ease with which the new information can move from the focus to the periphery of our attention. Technology designed with this in mind allows the user to easily move in and out of a state of flow, working at peak performance while avoiding techno-stress. That is what Weiser called Calm Technology.

Keywords HCI · Calm technology · Flow · Peripheral interaction · Techno-stress · ABC · Smart homes · Wise home

3.1 Calm Technology: "...As Refreshing as Taking a Walk in the Woods"

In 1991, Professor Mark Weiser wrote that "Machines that fit the human environment instead of forcing humans to enter theirs will make using a computer as refreshing as taking a walk in the woods" [1]. Current issues with interoperability, product design and human factors prevent Smart Home users from being able to see the forest for the trees, but this does not have to be the case. As mentioned earlier, Professor Weiser coined the term "Ubiquitous Computing" (UC) and theorized that it would eventually lead to an era of "Calm Technology" (CT) wherein computers would be embedded not only in our devices, but in our lives as well. As he put it:

> ...the most profound technologies are those that disappear. They weave themselves into the pattern of everyday life until they are indistinguishable from it. [1]

Calm Technology is based on the way that humans process information: the process of plucking things from the periphery and deciding how to prioritize them is a comforting activity that makes us feel at home and in control. Weiser and Brown provided examples of calm output from a network, but did not provide examples of calm input. That said, it seems logical that calm input would be based on the natural means of human to human communication. This requires a greater depth of multimodality than has previously been common.

© The Author(s) 2017
J.N.A. Brown et al., *Building an Intuitive Multimodal Interface for a Smart Home*,
Human–Computer Interaction Series, DOI 10.1007/978-3-319-56532-3_3

3.2 Understanding Calm

Calm Technology describes any tool that can be used with uninterrupted focus on a central task while new outside information is easily perceived and processed peripherally [2]. This dynamic allows the user to decide whether to divert their attention and change their focus at any time. This is the natural means by which all primates interact with their environment [3], and it is a fundamental part of the iterative cycles of perception, evaluation, and reaction that have shaped our evolution and that continue to shape our understanding of, and interaction with, the world around us [4]. Furthermore, Calm Technology allows one to focus on their intended action rather than on the tool they are using [5].

The concept of Calm Interaction is often misunderstood as a means of calming the user, as at The Stanford Calming Technology Lab, and in Rogers' call to abandon the concept in favour of "engaging rather than calming people" [6]. As mentioned earlier, "Calm" has also been conflated with the automation of decision processes, as exemplified by Makonin et al. [7], Olaru et al. [8], and Stavropoulos et al. [9], despite the obvious fact that automated decisions remove control from the user rather than simplifying it.

The problem that "Calm" is intended to address is the problem of enabling people to deal with large amounts of information without becoming either overwhelmed by stress or oblivious to the world around them.

3.3 Is "Calm" Necessary?

Csikszentmihalyi's concept of flow [10] has been used to describe situations in which the demands of task performance so coincide with the abilities of the performer as to enhance performance rather than limiting it. This total immersion might sound like calm, but it should not be confused with "Calm" in the sense that Weiser described it. Being in "flow" reduces one's ability to perceive or interact with the rest of the world [11].

Santangelo, Fagioli and Macaluso have described the natural processes by which the brain deals with large amounts of multimodal information [12]. Our ability to deal with interruptions has been discussed extensively for most of the last century, with informative analysis of the processes and the stresses involved provided by Zeigarnik, in 1927 [13] and by Gillie and Broadbent in 1987 [14].

According to Brod, techno-stress comes from feeling overwhelmed by information and options which are not fully understood [15]. Riedl et al. confirmed this by measuring the presence of stress hormones in saliva, and proposed that this stress can be mitigated by developing a feeling of being in control [16].

It was Weiser and Brown who suggested that the natural means by which humans sort and prioritize information in their natural environment could be the remedy for the stressful environment created by UC [5]. They postulated that following natural processes of prioritization would allow humans to feel more at ease and even to distinguish between natural situations that should or should not be classed as legitimately stressful. It seems logical to infer that deliberately-designed interactions could be created in a manner that is free of unnecessary or unproductive stress.

We have proposed, in an earlier work, practical examples of "Calm" in modern computer interaction; input and output systems based on human information processing rather than machine processing [17, 18]. While this has been discussed theoretically for some time, by the likes of Polanyi [19], Popper [20], Cadiz et al. [21], and van Dantzich et al. [22], it has led to very few practical examples. Weiser and Brown suggested examples from the analog world, like semi-opaque inner-office windows [5]. Virolainen et al. suggested HCI devices [23] and Bakker et al. created peripheral interaction devices to help students track the passage of time [24] and to help teachers photo-document student activities in the classroom.

References

1. Weiser M (1991) The computer for the twenty-first century. Sci Am 265(3):94–104 (Macmillan, New York)
2. Weiser M, Brown JS (1996) Designing calm technology. PowerGrid J 1(1):75–85
3. Brown JNA (2013) It's as easy as ABC: introducing anthropology-based computing. In: Advances in computational intelligence. Springer, Heidelberg, pp 1–16
4. Crapse TB, Sommer MA (2008) Corollary discharge across the animal kingdom. Nat Rev Neurosci 9(8):587–600
5. Weiser M, Brown JS (1997) The coming age of calm technology. In: Denning PJ, Metcalfe RM (eds) Beyond calculation: the next fifty years of computing. Copernicus, New York, pp 75–85
6. Rogers Y (2006) Moving on from weiser's vision of calm computing: engaging ubicomp experiences. In: UbiComp 2006: ubiquitous computing. Springer, Heidelberg, pp 404–421
7. Makonin S, Bartram L, Popowich F (2012) Redefining the "smart" in smart home: case studies of ambient intelligence
8. Olaru A, Florea AM, El Fallah Seghrouchni A (2012) A context-aware multi-agent system as a middleware for ambient intelligence. Mob Netw Appl 1–15
9. Stavropoulos TG, Vrakas D, Vlachava D, Bassiliades N (2013) BOnSAI: a smart building ontology for ambient intelligence. In: Proceedings of the 2nd International Conference on Web Intelligence, Mining and Semantics. p 30
10. Nakamura J, Csikszentmihalyi M (2002) The concept of flow. In: Handbook of positive psychology. pp 89–105
11. Csikszentmihalyi M, Bennett S (1971) An exploratory model of play. Am Anthropol 73 (1):45–58
12. Santangelo V, Fagioli S, Macaluso E (2010) The costs of monitoring simultaneously two sensory modalities decrease when dividing attention in space. Neuroimage 49:2717–2727
13. Zeigarnik B (1927) On the retention of completed and uncompleted activities. Psychologische Forschung 9:1–85
14. Gilbreth FB (1912) Primer of scientific management. D. Van Nostrand Company
15. Brod C (1984) Technostress: the human cost of the computer revolution. Addison-Wesley, Reading

16. Riedl R, Kindermann H, Auinger A, Javor A (2012) Technostress from a neurobiological perspective. Bus Inf Syst Eng 1–9
17. Brown JNA, Leitner G, Hitz M, Català Mallofré A (2014) A model of calm HCI. In: Bakker S, Hausen D, Selker T, van den Hoven E, Butz A, Eggen B (eds) Peripheral Interaction: shaping the research and design space. Workshop at CHI2014, Toronto, Canada. ISSN: 1862-5207
18. Brown JNA, Bayerl PS, Fercher A, Leitner G, Català Mallofré A, Hitz M (2014) A measure of calm. In: Bakker S, Hausen D, Selker T, van den Hoven E, Butz A, Eggen B (eds) Peripheral interaction: shaping the research and design space. Workshop at CHI2014, Toronto, Canada. ISSN: 1862-5207
19. Polanyi M (1962) Personal knowledge: towards a post-critical philosophy. Psychology Press
20. Popper KR (1972) Objective knowledge: an evolutionary approach. Clarendon Press, Oxford
21. Cadiz JJ, Venolia G, Jancke G, Gupta A (2002) Designing and deploying an information awareness interface. In: Proceedings of the 2002 ACM conference on Computer supported cooperative work. ACM, pp 314–323
22. Van Dantzich M, Robbins D, Horvitz E, Czerwinski M (2002) Scope: providing awareness of multiple notifications at a glance. In: Proceedings of the Working Conference on Advanced Visual Interfaces. ACM, pp 267–281
23. Virolainen A, Puikkonen A, Kärkkäinen T, Häkkilä J (2010) Cool interaction with calm technologies: experimenting with ice as a multitouch surface. In: ACM International Conference on Interactive Tabletops and Surfaces. pp 15–18
24. Bakker S, van den Hoven E, Eggen B (2012) Acting by hand: informing interaction design for the periphery of people's attention. Interact Comput 24:119–130

Chapter 4
"What I Tell You Three Times Is True": The S.N.A.R.K. Circuit

Abstract So-called natural interaction with smart homes has been limited by a misunderstanding of how humans naturally interact. Consider speech. Chatbots, developed to push the limits of voice-based interaction ignore the fact that natural human speech is actually multi-modal, supplemented both consciously and unconsciously by posture, gesture, facial expression, and a complex web of flexible situational data. In terms of UX design, this is not a bug but a feature. The inability of voice-based systems to recognize spoken commands can be corrected by using additional natural signals such as gestures, to increase the signal-to-noise ratio. This form of modular redundancy was fundamental to early satellite communications and became the basis for our S.N.A.R.K. Circuit, the means by which a human with the correct mental model can interact intuitively with a Smart Home.

Keywords Smart home · Calm technology · Multimodal interaction · Chatbots · Triple modular redundancy · Mental models · Bellman's protocol · B.O.O.J.U.M. · S.N.A.R.K. circuit · "The Hunting of the Snark"

Our intent has been to create a system that would allow users to speak naturally with their Smart Home. Since the idea was first proposed formally by Weizenbaum in 1966, chatbots have gone in two directions [1]. They either intended to fool humans into believing that the Turing test [2] has been passed (here we get conversational patterns based on a misunderstanding of Rogerian psychotherapeutic questioning [3]), or they are designed to elicit expected responses from a pre-determined database of choices (here we are subject to the prejudices of recommender systems, designed to believe that they know what the user wants—either in general or in specific—better than the user does, herself). The prototypes of the pseudo chatbot used in our studies were built based on existing open-source engines, but were not be trained to "keep the conversation going at all costs" or to "help the user find her way to one of the available solutions." The intent of this pseudo-chatbox is to conversationally encourage the user to express their own ideas in a relaxed and natural manner, simulating the conversation two friendly humans might share when they are working together in a strict but informal chain of command. The version we used was intended to work the same way, but also to assist in the illusion that the user is interacting with a single holistic entity, rather than a network of embedded systems.

In 2013, Brown evaluated whether or not a speech and sound recognition software similar to the one described above can be made to work in an acoustically hostile environment, given the addition of a simple command protocol [4]. This protocol is based on the triple-modular-redundancy systems common to engineering, a truly user-centered perspective, and a hundred year old nonsense poem in which the captain tells his crew: "I tell you three times, it must be true" [5].

4.1 A New Paradigm Part 1—The Bellman's Protocol

The underlying concept of Martial Arts training is that, through preparation, one can better deal with any situation that one can anticipate. In this manner, the difficulty of figuring out what to do and how to do it is chronologically displaced [6]. The Chinese socio-cultural teachings that predate this attitude were addressed by Brown in a plenary session lecture at ICME 2012 [7]. In that talk, Brown proposed that, in the same way that this level of preparation prevents the martial artists from having to consider each new challenge individually, designers, programmers and engineers should be able to anticipate every use of their tools, and so should be able to make interaction less demanding at the moment of use.

As summarized by Nass and Moon [8], there is a lot of data proposing that humans accidentally and unconsciously interact with machines according to protocols established in human-human interaction. Surely this could be the key to making HCI intuitive and mindless. The user needs to have a familiar mental model to justify their input behaviors.

4.2 A New Paradigm Part 2—The B.O.O.J.U.M

A standard, generic lexicon and ontology will not allow the user to work within the personally-defined parameters of a mental model, requiring instead that the user(s) adapt themselves to their environment, in direct opposition to Weiser's intent.

The B.O.O.J.U.M. (Brown's Open Ontology for Joint User Management) allows each individual user to use their own preferred commands and names for each device, and is made up of two parts. The first is a device ontology based on formally recording the common values in each user's mental map of their home. This does not require any changes to the underlying ontology of the networked and embedded systems in the home; it is intended to assist the users, not the software. The second part of the B.O.O.J.U.M. is a 20-item command lexicon derived from a survey of 435 atomic use cases based on activities of daily living (ADL) which will be discussed in the next section of this chapter.

The question becomes how to enable the computer to perceive the subtle signals that would reflect the mental model from which they are working, and the answer is surprising: concurrent signals conveying the same meaning improve accuracy of data transfer.

4.3 A New Paradigm Part 3—The S.N.A.R.K. Circuit

We proposed the *S.N.A.R.K. Circuit*, an early step towards a new paradigm of smart home interaction [9]. Our goal is to provide a solution to the problem of using audio signals and voice commands in a noisy environment: a system that will wait unobtrusively to be called into service.

Figure 4.1 shows the *S.N.A.R.K. Circuit*, a "tell-me-three-times" command redundancy protocol or *Triple Modular Redundancy* [10] designed to fill the black box often assigned to filter noise from intentional command. Ideally, the trigger should be one that is easy to perform intentionally but difficult to perform accidentally. Conceptually, these parameters could be used to describe most naturally multimodal communication used by humans [11]; the combination of voice with the "separate symbolic vehicle" that we call gesture [12]. These can be simple actions such as using the space between one's thumb and forefinger to illustrate the size of an object while also describing it verbally. An ambiguous gesture can be easily misunderstood. For example, waving one's hands loosely in the air may mean several different things; from cheering in formal sign language to cooling burnt fingers, from saying hello to saying goodbye. Other gestures are less likely to occur by accident.

Our chosen example is the double clap. Clapping an uncounted number of times may be common, but clapping twice is well understood to be a means of getting attention from either a group or an individual. As a gesture, clapping twice is quite unique, in that it involves limited inverted movements coming immediately one

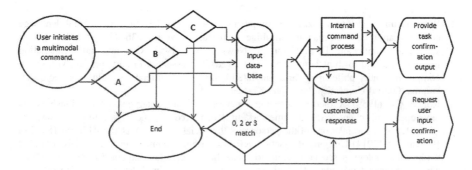

Fig. 4.1 The S.N.A.R.K. Circuit: where any 3 recognized commands (*A, B, C*), detected within a small space of time, are compared to see if they hold the same meaning. If two of the recognized commands match, user confirmation is sought. If three match, the command is generated

after the other, and it is clearly delimited by a rapid start and equally sudden stop. This was established in an earlier study in which 16 participants performed double claps recognized by a smartphone affixed to their arm as a step in multi-modal interaction [13]. After the main trial was completed, each participant was asked to try to perform some movement that the software and hardware might mistake for a double clap.

> Despite some wonderful performances, 75% of the participants were unable to deliberately generate a false positive. Two participants succeeded by vigorously shaking hands. Two others attempted to fool the system by doing the chicken dance. Only one of the dancers was successful.

While many people are familiar with the decades-old technology of double-clap sound recognition used as a comically-unreliable on/off switch for electrical devices, this is not what we are proposing. We are proposing that the sound and the movement of the double-clap both be used as independent signals which can make up two of the three inputs recognizable and useable in our triple redundancy. This introduces one aspect of Calm Technology in that the user, intending to produce the noise of a double clap inadvertently produces the movement recognized as a separate signal. Inadvertent communication with a computerized system through natural human behavior is one of the key aspects of Calm Technology [14].

The trigger should also allow the system to distinguish known users from one another and from strangers. In "The Hunting of the Snark" Lewis Carroll wrote: "I tell you three times, it must be true!" [5]. We propose that a passive system could become active when triggered by three roughly simultaneous commands of equivalent meaning, delivered in different modalities. All three signals can be produced via the execution of a common human behavior for getting the attention of subordinates—the motion and sound of a double clap paired with the sound of a spoken name…

References

1. Weizenbaum J (1966) ELIZA—a computer program for the study of natural language communication between man and machine. Commun ACM 9(1a):36–45
2. Turing A, Braithwaite R, Jefferson G, Newman, M (1952) Can automatic calculating machines be said to think? In: Copeland BJ (ed) The essential turing: seminal writings in computing, logic, philosophy, artificial intelligence, and artificial life: plus the secrets of enigma, Oxford University Press, pp 487–506
3. Rogers CR (1959) A theory of therapy, personality, and interpersonal relationships: as developed in the client-centered framework. In: Koch S (ed) Psychology: a study of a science. Study 1, vol 3: formulations of the person and the social context. McGraw-Hill, pp 184–256
4. Brown JNA (2014) Unifying interaction across distributed controls in a smart environment: using anthropology-based computing to make human-computer interaction "calm". Ph.D. Thesis. Erasmus Mundus Joint Doctorate Programme in Interactive and Cognitive Environments, Alpen-Adria-Universität Klagenfurt, and Universitat Politècnica de Catalunya
5. Carroll L (1876) The Hunting of the Snark. Macmillan, London

6. Brown JNA (2011) Martial arts. In: Greenwald SJ, Thomley JE (eds) Encyclopedia of mathematics and society. Salem Press, Hackensack
7. Brown JNA (2012) Expert talk for time machine session: designing calm technology "... as refreshing as taking a walk in the woods". 2012 IEEE international conference on multimedia and expo, vol 1, p 423
8. Nass C, Moon Y (2000) Machines and mindlessness: social responses to computers. J Soc Issues 56(1):81–103
9. Brown JNA, Leitner G, Hitz M, Català Mallofré A (2014) A model of calm HCI. In: Peripheral interaction: shaping the research and design space, workshop at CHI, vol 24
10. Kaschmitter JL, Shaeffer DL, Colella NJ, McKnett CL, Coakley PG (1991) Operation of commercial R3000 processors in the low earth orbit (LEO) space environment. IEEE Trans Nucl Sci 38(6):1415–1420
11. Ennis C, McDonnell R, O'Sullivan C (2010) Seeing is believing: body motion dominates in multisensory conversations. ACM Trans Graph 29(4):91
12. McNeill D (1992) Hand and mind: what gestures reveal about thought. University of Chicago Press, Chicago
13. Brown JNA, Kaufmann B, Huber FJ, Pirolt K H, Hitz M (2013) "... Language in their very gesture" first steps towards calm smart home input. In: Human-computer interaction and knowledge discovery in complex, unstructured, big data. Springer, Berlin Heidelberg, pp 256–264
14. Weiser M, Brown JS (1997) The coming age of calm technology. In: Denning PJ, Metcalfe RM (eds) Beyond calculation: the next fifty years of computing. Copernicus, New York, pp 75–85

Chapter 5
"Do All that You Know, and Try All that You Don't...": Models of Intuitive Interaction

Abstract Humans perceive the world not as it is, but as we imagine it. Specifically, we do not process what we perceive in real time. Instead we make irregular updates to a mental model of the world around us, and it is that mental model with which we interact. In order to interact successfully with any environment, we need to have a functional mental model. We created two mental models for use with our S.N.A.R.K. Circuit, mental models that would relieve the user from having to understand complicated details about the interaction. This moved the process to their unconscious and made it more intuitive. The original goal of this project was to induce in the user a mental model of the home as a single entity, by enabling multi-modal interaction and easy transfer between modalities and devices. In order to achieve intuitiveness, we moved the goalposts. Giving voice commands to an invisible major domo, or waving your smart phone like a wand do not reflect normal life, but do reflect interactions that are already well-accepted enough to be intuitive.

Keywords Smart homes · Calm technology · CASA TEVA · Multimodal inter-action · Intuitive interaction · SNARK circuit, mental models

Each individual participant was introduced to the setting and involved in a brief discussion of home controls, in order to establish whether or not they already had a mental model of butlers and house servants. The C.A.S.A. T.E.V.A. app was then introduced and the participant was informed that they now had their own digital head butler who would act as their personal intermediary to help get things done around the house. They were each asked to name their personal digital butler (Fig. 5.1), and introduced to one of the two methods of interacting with this invisible servant.

The first interaction $(m_v,)$, based principally on voice, involved clapping to get the attention of the invisible butler and then speaking simple commands of your own choice. As will be shown, this interaction was centered on voice, but involved other modalities in peripheral but important roles.

© The Author(s) 2017

J.N.A. Brown et al., *Building an Intuitive Multimodal Interface for a Smart Home*, Human–Computer Interaction Series, DOI 10.1007/978-3-319-56532-3_5

Fig. 5.1 The participant
could name their invisible
butler

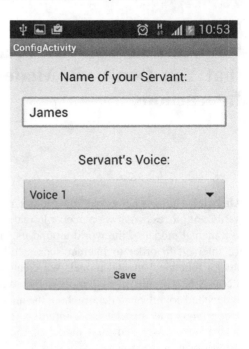

The second method of interacting with the invisible butler (m_g,) was centered around treating one's phone like a magic wand, and waving it in a simple gesture while saying the name of the device you wanted to control.

Let us more closely examine the underlying mental models and user experience involved in both methods.

5.1 The Voice-Centered Method

The first manifestation (m_v) is centered on spoken communication between the user and the digital assistant. Visual displays assist the user with their timing and with immediate feedback on the success of the different stages of their attempt.

An interaction scenario proceeds as follows: The participant is seated in an easy chair against one wall of the room, as in Fig. 5.2, with the smartphone sitting on the table next to her. She double-claps her hands, in order to get the attention of the system, and she glances at the phone to see if it has reacted to that sound pattern

Fig. 5.2 m_v: voice-centered interaction

Fig. 5.3 Acknowledging the call to attention and asking which butler is being called

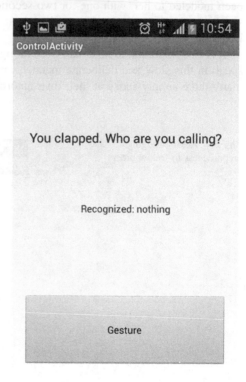

among the background noises. If it has, it signals her with written text, asking which butler she wishes to contact (Fig. 5.3). This response is only in writing because we did not want the participant to be annoyed by vocal queries caused by false positives.

With the right mental model in place, this would not have to be read, just seen as a change in the display. In fact, taking the time to read the words might delay the user too long for the next step to be successfully performed in the limited time allowed. If the participant feels comfortable enough with the system (as was often the case in our experiment) she does not try to read the message. We see this in the majority of first attempts where the participant does not lean in or take hold of the phone in order to read the text. In cases where the system did not work on the first attempt, then the participant was more likely to try to read the message. During the first attempt, the participant either goes forward based on her own internal timing or she allows a general perception of a change on the screen to cue her to speak the name she has assigned to her personal butler before testing began.

"James", she says, and pauses again in her speech. It is important to note that these are not breaks in her speech, but pauses. She is speaking in the way that it has been modeled to her, with one- or two-second delays between each phrase. She is speaking clearly and slowly, as though to someone who is just learning the language.

It is also important to note that, even though the participants were shown how to speak in this slow and deliberate manner, and even though many of them did so, many more simply spoke at their own natural speed.

Fig. 5.4 Acknowledging preparedness to follow orders

Fig. 5.5 Acknowledging the last command and preparedness for the next

Once the system has heard a recognized name, it queries the participant. In writing, a phrase appears on the screen: "How may I help you?", as illustrated in Fig. 5.4. James also speaks to her in a slow and friendly, very human voice. "What would you like me to do?"

Referring to her list of tasks, the participant sees "Turn on the light" and is reminded that she can use any normal English-language phrase that contains the keywords "turn on" and "light".

If James has understood, the desk lamp on the coffee table lights up and the on-screen text changes in case the participant needs a reminder that James can be summoned again (Fig. 5.5). If at any time, James has not understood, he apologizes in both writing and voice, verbally asking the participant to repeat her command (Fig. 5.6).

Fig. 5.6 Clarifying that the
last spoken command was not
understood

5.2 The Gesture-Centered Method

The second manifestation (m_g) is centered around gestural interaction, but with
required elements of speech- and GUI-based interaction as well. Again, written and
aural feedback helps to keep the user aware of the stages of the process. An
interaction scenario would proceed in the following manner.

5.2.1 Interaction Scenario

The participant is sitting or standing according to their preference. Several chose to
alternate sitting and standing or to walk around while performing the tasks. One
participant chose to lay down (Fig. 5.7). Since the phone is already at hand, the
participant presses the large button at the bottom of the ready screen labeled
"Gesture". In the next iteration, if the button is released after less than 0.5 s, the
signal will be discounted as an error. In the iteration that was tested, this results in a
spoken error message: "I'm sorry, were you trying to get me to do something? I

Fig. 5.7 One participant,
relaxed, during
gesture-centered interaction

didn't understand. Would you please repeat that action?" At the same time, the written word "Sorry" appears on-screen.

If the button stays depressed, the following message appears on the screen: "Please name the device." After a brief pause, the participant names the device he wants to control. If the sound detected is not recognized as a known device or command word, the same error messages described earlier appear again, in both text and speech. At the same time, another message appears at the bottom of the screen: "I think you said: (x)", where x is replaced by whatever word was understood by the system. This extra written message is intended to provide additional feedback to the participant, so that they can correct their speech, if needed. This is intended as a polite reflection of the way in which a human collocutor would repeat a word that was not understood.

If the name has been understood, then there is no interruption in either writing or speech. The participant then waves the phone in one of three gestures, releasing the button once the movement is complete. If the gesture is not understood, the same error messages described earlier appear again, in both text and speech, including the message at the bottom of the screen.

If the gesture is understood, then the device and action are both correctly named in the message at the bottom of the screen. One example would be: "You said "light, off". As the text appears, the command is carried out. The message relating to the last action remains visible at the bottom of the screen, even as the rest of the screen returns to ready status.

5.2.2   The Three Gestures

The three gestures used in our trial are derived from the 19 basic commands that were a product of an unpublished review of 435 elemental use cases in the home. These use cases could be grouped into 94 different categories based on their function, modality, location or purpose. In developing our set of gestures, it proved possible to combine several of the 19 basic commands into a single concept: state change. As discussed earlier, a gesture need not reflect a word from any particular human language. Even though "state change" is not a common command in the English language, it does describe the intent of a number of different paired/binary commands such as: "on/off" or "open/close".

This being the case, a single "state change" gesture could serve as well for opening or closing the blinds as it could for turning on or off the radio, the lights or even the air conditioner. The gesture itself was illustrated in a manner related to the gestural metaphor of a magic wand. As shown in Fig. 5.8, one need only imagine oneself a wizard with a wand in place of the phone in one's hand and then drop the tip of the wand in the manner familiar across cultures.

Two other gestures were necessary in order to carry out the last two of the nine tasks that made up our testing protocol. These are gestures for "more" and "less". Here again we deviate from the work of Hurtienne et al. [1] as discussed in Chap. 3. Rather than basing the gestures on an assumed universally-understood spatial relationship between the person and their perception of the world, we chose to base our gestures on a global metaphor which is, itself, based on a cultural metaphor (that exploits social signifiers [2]).

Volume sliders can be either vertical or horizontal. When horizontal, they increase from left to right, that is, in the same direction as word count in a written sentence—in most written languages. Even in cultures with languages traditionally written either right-to-left or vertically (Hebrew, Japanese, etc.), volume sliders universally work in the same direction.

Fig. 5.8 The mental model of using a magic wand, and the gesture for "state change"

Fig. 5.9 Mental model of *left*-to-*right* progression and the gestures for "less" and "more"

On this basis, our gesture for "more" was to move as though increasing volume on a slider or word count in a written phrase, that is; a horizontal movement to the right. Our gesture for "less" was the opposite: a horizontal movement leftward. These gestures, and the mental models from which they are derived, are illustrated in Fig. 5.9.

After performing the trial using one method, the participant was asked to start again using the other. The order was controlled, with 16 participants starting with each of the two manifestations.

The results of this experiment, and the implications thereof, are discussed in the following chapters.

References

1. Hurtienne J, Stößel C, Sturm C, Maus A, Rötting M, Langdon P, Clarkson J (2010) Physical gestures for abstract concepts: inclusive design with primary metaphors. Interact Comput 22 (6):475–484
2. Norman DA (2011) Living with complexity. The MIT Press, Cambridge, Massachusetts [u.a.]

Chapter 6
"The Method Employed I Would Gladly Explain...": Set up, Location and Protocol

Abstract In order to test the C.A.S.A. T.E.V.A. concept in the Casa Vecchia setting without disrupting the lives of the families living in our smart homes, we brought 38 international participants into a functional smart home lab based on the campus of the Alpen-Adria Universität Klagenfurt, in southern Austria. They were introduced to the system and asked to perform a series of tasks using some of the networked and embedded devices common to the Casa Vecchia homes. This chapter describes, in detail, the experimental setting and the test protocol.

Keywords Casa vecchia · C.A.S.A. T.E.V.A · Smart home · Study design · Experimental setting · Living lab · HCI · Daily household tasks · Smart home platform · Smart home technology · S.N.A.R.K · B.O.O.J.U.M

The Living Lab smart environment laboratory at Alpen-Adria-Universität Klagenfurt has an open ceiling, exposing the lab to the regular office noises of an active research center housing four research groups, their technicians and their administrative support on the floor above. Furthermore, another laboratory and a set of offices have access to the lab through two doors, and use the lab as a passageway. Finally, the lab itself includes a functional kitchen and bathroom, both of which are at the disposal of all of the workers in all of those other rooms. This gives us a constantly-changing ebb and flow of background noise, including single and multiple voices, machinery sounds and sometimes a radio. It is our intent to state that such everyday noises do not interfere with the use of our system, even though noises and voices are crucial components of our input protocol.

6.1 Participants

32 volunteers [17 men and 15 women, ranging in age from 17 to 47, with a median age of 27 (8.29)] participated in a test of the two multimodal methodologies for interacting with our new, holistic and intuitive smartphone-based smart home

© The Author(s) 2017
J.N.A. Brown et al., *Building an Intuitive Multimodal Interface for a Smart Home*, Human–Computer Interaction Series, DOI 10.1007/978-3-319-56532-3_6

Fig. 6.1 The living lab at Alpen-Adria-Universität Klagenfurt as seen through our surveillance camera

interface. They were recorded and monitored unobtrusively from another room (Fig. 6.1).

Our original cohort numbered 38. As in Cook et al. [1], some recruits (two male and one female) had to be removed from our study for not following the experimental protocol.

Each participant filled out pre- and post-trial questionnaires, supplying us with their demographic data and with qualitative feedback regarding their experience. The results compiled from these qualitative questionnaires are addressed later.

6.2 Familiarization

Interacting with computers has always required some new, learned behavior on the part of the user, whether it is the use of punch cards or trackballs, Fortran or Java. Here, based on the Bellman's Protocol, we reverse the usual HCI paradigm requiring the adjustment of the user's skill set to suit the needs of the system. For that reason, it was expected that our system should be useful without familiarization. Participants were instructed in the basic methodology and given a written sheet describing the order of the tasks and the means of performing them. These descriptions were written in English. The participants were not given enough time or practice to familiarize themselves with the system [2].

Instead, the participants were each engaged in a discussion of the history of personal servants, and told how the development of electric switches transferred the responsibility of performing some tasks away from the serving class and on to technology. In this way the participants were introduced to a mental model of their own homes populated by invisible servants waiting to be told to perform electronic tasks. This led into the suggestion that, here in the Living Lab, they could use an invisible *major domo* or *lead butler* to manage all of the invisible servants.

6.3 Testing Protocol

Each participant was presented with a list of nine simple household tasks that would usually require a mixture of absolute and scalar controls on four distributed mechanical devices. These devices were set up in the test space shown in Fig. 6.2, some in plain view and others invisible to the participant. They were told that they would be asked to: (1) Turn on the light in front of them; (2) Turn off the light in front of them; (3) Turn on the Air Conditioner they cannot see; (4) Turn on the Radio that they can hear from the next room; (5) Turn off the radio that they can hear from the next room; (6) Open the blinds next to them; (7) Close the blinds next to them; (8) Open those same blinds a little more, and; (9) Close those same blinds a little more.

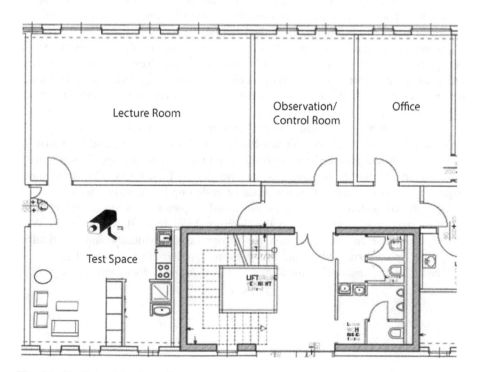

Fig. 6.2 The living lab schematic

6.4 Technological Set up

Home automation functions for the household tasks were implemented on the basis of a Smart Home middleware platform which was originally developed in-house for the Casa Vecchia [3] project. The OSGi [4] based platform provides a flexible service oriented architecture to easily support different Smart Home hardware devices via specific driver services as well as implementations for various input and output modalities. The hardware foundation in the living lab constitutes a wireless home automation system (Homematic [5]) enabling the remote control of appliances included in our test scenarios through the Casa Vecchia middleware platform. The middleware and the home automation system are interconnected with each other over a XML-RPC [6] interface.

The C.A.S.A T.E.V.A. app is implemented in Android on API level 2.3, the access to the Casa Vecchia Smart Home middleware is realized with a SOAP based Webservice interface.

Clap detection is implemented with the help of musicg [7]—a lightweight open source sound analysis library that also supports natural sound detection based on data gathered from Android's audio recording service. To distinguish double claps from single ones and most other similar natural environmental noises, the interval between two claps has to lie between 400 and 2000 ms.

For speech recognition we used the built-in online speech recognition service of the Android platform as it provided adequate recognition rates without the need for our participants to go through individual training sessions to optimize the recognition engine. Language settings are set to U.S. English and the maximum results per query to the recognition engine were limited to five. Results from the speech recognition service are compared to the contents of a prepared dictionary containing servant names as well as device names together with their respective action commands.

Gesture recognition is realized on the basis of an open source recognition library (Wiigee [8]) which employs a hidden Markov model for training and recognizing gestures from data provided by the Android phone's accelerometer. Gestures that our participants used were trained in advance by staff members. The anticipated negative impact on user/system performance ended up being insignificant.

Speech and gesture inputs can be processed in parallel. Fusion of speech and gesture commands takes place on the decision level [e.g. 9] which means that gestures and speech command first are recognized individually and are finally combined into a command for the Smart Home middleware in a second step.

The internal state model of the C.A.S.A. T.E.V.A app is documented in Fig. 6.3.

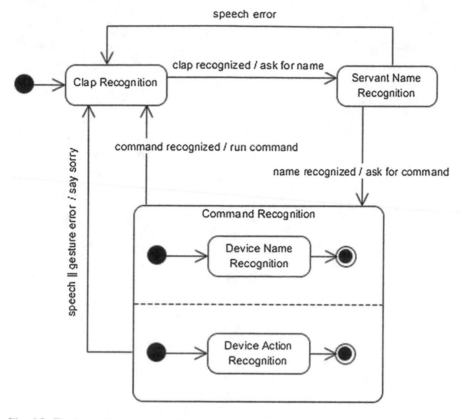

Fig. 6.3 The internal state model of the C.A.S.A. T.E.V.A. app

References

1. Cook DJ, Das SK (2012) Pervasive computing at scale: transforming the state of the art. Pervasive Mob Comput 8(1):22–35
2. Dainoff M, Haber RN (1967) How much help do repeated presentations give to recognition processes? Percept Psychophys 2(4):131–136
3. Leitner G, Fercher A, Felfernig A, Hitz M (2012) Reducing the entry threshold of AAL systems: preliminary results from casa vecchia. In: Miesenberger K, Karshmer A, Penaz P, Zagler W (eds) Computers helping people with special needs lecture notes in computer science, vol 7382, 1st edn. Springer, Heidelberg, pp 709–715
4. https://www.osgi.org
5. http://www.homematic.com
6. http://xmlrpc.scripting.com
7. https://github.com/loisaidasam/musicg
8. http://www.wiigee.org
9. Pantic M, Rothkrantz LJM (2003) Toward an affect-sensitive multimodal human-computer interaction. Proc IEEE 91(9):1370–1390

Chapter 7
"...They Are Merely Conventional Signs...": Measuring Intuitive Interaction

Abstract C.A.S.A. T.E.V.A. strives for the unification of a heterogeneous network with seamless switching between devices and intuitive interaction. Two mental models were put forward, each to enable intuitive multimodal interaction centered on either voice or gesture. The user could give voice commands to an invisible major domo, or could wave their smart phone like a wand while calling out the names of devices like magic spells. Our goal was not simply to build a multimodal interface, but to build one that was intuitive. This would necessitate the ability to measure intuitiveness. To do so we developed a protocol of measuring whether or not the participants could intuit how to use the recently-introduced but still unfamiliar system to perform new tasks. Any task that required more than three immediately-consecutive attempts was considered a failure.

Keywords C.A.S.A. T.E.V.A. · Mental models · HCI · Intuitive interaction · Multimodal interaction · Smart homes · Metrics · Gestural interaction · Voice interaction · Casa vecchia · Calm technology · Flow

The new interaction paradigm, as expressed in our C.A.S.A. T.E.V.A. app, is an attempt to unify the control of a network of heterogeneous systems. The intent was to make transition from the control of one device to the control of another intuitive, and to make the transition from one modality to another seamless. Finally, we hoped to create in our participants the perception of the home as a single holistic entity. The conceptual basis for this has been described above. The attempted measurement of it is described below.

7.1 Intuitive Transition Between Devices

The intuitive transition from controlling one device to controlling another was created by using a single perceptual and interactional ontology to control all devices. In this way, initiating a state change in one device required the participant to use the same behavior as when initiating a state change in any other device. This allowed the participant to work across devices following a single, holistic mental model.

This was tested by foregoing the usual protocol of familiarization. This lack of familiarization forced each participant to decide on their own how to transfer what they had learned about controlling one device to the task of controlling the other devices. If the participant did so on the first attempt, then intuitive transition had been successfully achieved.

Thus, the outcome measure for intuitive transfer is the ability of the participant to perform all nine of the tasks using the different systems embedded in our network. This will be discussed, and conclusions will be drawn, in later chapters of this book.

7.2   Seamless Transfer Between Modalities

The seamless transfer from one modality to another is, as discussed in Chap. 2, a naturally-occurring element of human communication, so long as the modalities are used in combination. Conversely, the use of a single modality is artificial and occurs only in response to a situation that prohibits natural communication.

Scuba diving requires single-modality communication (gestural interaction), as does use of a traditional telephone or two-way radio (vocal interaction). Our system attempts to recreate the rich multi-modal interaction that is intuitive to humans. This is done with the use of more than one modality, even when a single modality is the principle focus of interaction. This gives us two separate outcome measures for the seamless transition between modalities.

The first is the ability of the participant to transfer knowledge of how to perform a task using the gesture-centered manifestation of our app to performing the same task using a speech-centered manifestation, and vice versa.

The second outcome measure for the seamless transition between modalities is based on multimodality within each manifestation. More specifically, when using the speech-based manifestation of our app, the participant gets feedback aurally, but may also access additional information just by noticing that the screen layout has changed or by reading two different texts that appears on the screen.

The first one is a rephrasing of the aural message. The second one is a meta-level message, telling the participant "I think you said...". This gives the participant a deeper insight into why an interaction either worked or didn't, in much the same way that subtle facial or postural cues or word repetitions inform interlocutors during a human-human interaction. When using the gesture-centered manifestation of our app, feedback is also offered aurally, in writing, and as graphical change on the interface screen.

Thus, the ability to seamlessly accept feedback from multiple modalities is necessary in order to improve one's performance at a single task, and the outcome measure for this improvement is an increase in performance success as a task is repeated. For this reason, we evaluate performance in two ways.

The basic quantitative results given below were calculated on the basis that success at a first attempt was a pass and everything else was a failure. As mentioned above, this allowed us to test intuitiveness. However, we also collected comparative data considering success on first, second or third attempts. Improvement in performance as a result of feedback across modalities is the outcome measure for seamless transition between modalities within specific tasks. This is reflected in the comparison of performance in the first attempt to performance over the first three attempts. The conclusions we can draw on this basis are presented in Chap. 8.

7.3 Perception of the Home as a Single, Holistic Entity

The norm for smart home controls, as discussed in Chap. 2, is based on the concept that each device in the home has been grouped, in one way or another, into an ontological structure.

These ontological structures then become the templates for mental models that must be assumed by the user. For an example, let us consider the location of the "print" command in a word processing software. In order to print a document, you must first open the document, and then navigate to the control that allows you to choose the settings for the print job. In most standard software this navigation can be accomplished via icon, via cascading drop-down menu or via hot key. To use any of these paths requires an understanding of where the "print" command sits within the ontology of the system. In other words, the user must learn how to navigate to the command that will enable them to attempt to achieve their goal of issuing the command to print.

The underlying function of the Bellman's Protocol and the B.O.O.J.U.M., is to turn this navigational demand on its head. As discussed in earlier chapters, our C.A.S.A. T.E.V.A. app is not the first to propose a virtual major domo, but it is to our knowledge the first working version to do so for the express purpose of eliminating the navigational demands of HCI.

In the C.A.S.A. T.E.V.A. system, one does not have to navigate from the entertainment system database to the lighting system database, or from one room's control menu to the control menu for another room. In our system it is only necessary to identify the device and the action. It is the responsibility of our major domo to carry out your intent. If the major domo does not understand your intent, it is their responsibility to clearly and politely ask for more information using customized phrases and terminology from the B.O.O.J.U.M. In future iterations, recommender technologies or some other forms of artificial intelligence might provide a good addition or even a prerequisite to this system. For example, based on the location information of the smartphone (or the "Humantenna" technology that tracks a person's location within their home [1, 2]), or based on other contextual information, such as time of day and the "rituals" of the person, the system could "recommend" the device that the user might be more likely to use. In this way, and following the idea of having a hybrid set of recommender technologies as proposed in [3], the basic technologies really support users rather than overruling them.

The perception of the home as a single, holistic entity was measured using anthropological methods for impartial observation and application of logical reasoning to the observed facts. Conclusions drawn from the observed performance will be described in Chap. 9.

7.4   Data Extraction and Analysis

In order to differentiate between true and false positives and between true and false negatives, performance was judged by system records and also by video observation.

For our experiment, observers followed the trials during the live performance via audio and video transmission to another room. After the trials, three observers rated each attempted performance into one of four categories as explained here:

- True positive, where an attempt was made to perform a task, the attempt was well-executed, and the result was successfully detected;
- True negative, where an attempt was made to perform a task, the attempt was not, for one reason or another, executed successfully and the attempt was not detected by the system;
- False positive, where either no attempt was made, or the attempt was poorly executed, and yet the system reacted as though an attempt had been executed successfully, and;
- False negative, where an attempt was well-executed and yet, for one reason or another, was not understood by the system.

In order to increase the likelihood of the accuracy of these categorizations, the video record of each trial was reviewed independently by three observers. Each was familiar with the protocol, with the tasks, with the setting and hardware, and with the device. Each observer was familiarized with this procedure in a pilot trial. Working at their own pace and in separate locations, each observer took descriptive notes for each performance and made a judgment—either assigning one of the four rankings for each attempt, or taking note of an inability to do so. After all videos had been judged by each observer, the three met and reviewed their results.

If two or three of the observers agreed on an outcome, the outcome was accepted as accurate. If there was no consensus at all on what had happened, the video was re-watched by all three observers together and discussed. This discussion continued until consensus was reached.

References

1. Cohn G, Morris D, Patel SN, Tan DS (2011) Your noise is my command: sensing gestures using the body as an antenna. In: Proceedings of the 2011 annual conference on human factors in computing systems, vol 1. ACM, pp 791–800
2. Cohn G, Morris D, Patel SN, Tan DS (2012) Humantenna: using the body as an antenna for real-time whole-body interaction. In: Proceedings of the 2011 annual conference on human factors in computing systems
3. Leitner G, Ferrara F, Felfernig A, Tasso C (2011) Decision support in the smart home. In: RecSys workshop on human decision making in recommender systems, pp 8–16

Chapter 8
"How Do You Do?": Quantitative Results

Abstract Our multimodal interaction is based on a smartphone app that combines GUI, text, gestures and voice commands as a step towards intuitive human communication with a smart home. Shown how to perform two tasks, 32 participants were asked to intuit how to perform seven other tasks using networked and embedded devices through intuitive multimodal interaction based on universal mental models. 1st attempts were between 28.1 and 90.6% successful. By the third consecutive attempt, successes ranged from 65.6% on one device, to 100% on four others.

Keywords C.A.S.A. T.E.V.A. · HCI · Intuitive interaction · Multimodal interaction · Smart homes · Metrics · Gesture-centered interaction · Voice-centered interaction · Casa vecchia · Calm technology · Quantitative methods

Participants used both the gesture-centered method (m_g) and the voice-centered method (m_v) of multimodal interaction to perform 9 tasks. Descriptive analysis shows a mean success rate of 55.95% (28.13–68.75%) on *first* attempts performed with the voice-centered method, and a mean success rate of 64.84% (34.38–90.63%) when performed with the gesture-centered method. By the *third* attempt, success rates have climbed to a mean of 87.1% (65.6–100%) for the voice-centered method, with a median score of 90.6%. The gesture-centered method has resulted in a mean success rate of 91.6% (78.1–100%) with a median score of 93.8%.

For now, let us examine the results of the first attempts more closely.

8.1 First Attempts: A High Standard of Failure

The 32 participants performed the nine tasks using both the voice-centered (m_v) and gesture-centered (m_g) multimodal interaction methods. The results were analyzed using two-tailed, paired student's t-Tests conducted at 95% confidence level ($p <= 0.05$) in all but three cases.

© The Author(s) 2017
J.N.A. Brown et al., *Building an Intuitive Multimodal Interface for a Smart Home*,
Human–Computer Interaction Series, DOI 10.1007/978-3-319-56532-3_8

One participant did not perform task 1 ("turn on the light") and task 2 ("turn off the light"), and another did not perform task 7 ("close the blinds"). Since the number of performances to be incorporated into our calculations was not uniform for those tasks, the values for tasks 1, 2 and 7 were calculated using different sample sizes.

Looking at mean success rates based on first attempts by the total pool of participants, there is no significant difference between success rates (pass/fail ratios) based on the method used in seven out of the nine tasks (Table 8.1).

First attempts at these tasks using the gestural method of interaction both averaged 90.63%, well above average for m_g (64.8%). Table 8.2 shows that order had no significant effect on the voice centered method.

As seen in Table 8.3, the order of method use also had no significant effect on the success rate for the gesture-centered method.

The mean success rate of each task by all participants is shown in Fig. 8.1. Three tasks were attempted by only 31 participants. In all other cases task performance values were calculated from a base of 32 participants.

Please note that, as indicated in Table 8.1 (asterisk), the fourth and fifth tasks were performed with an uncharacteristic degree of success when compared with the other tasks. Please note also that the final task was performed with an uncharacteristically poor rate of success regardless of method, while the eighth task was almost as badly performed using the gesture-centered methodology.

The last two tasks (t8 "open the blinds more" and t9 "open the blinds less") were more conceptually difficult than the others. These scalar qualities of "more" and "less" required the use of new gestural commands, considerably different from the "state change" gesture used to perform the other tasks.

In terms of voice-centered interaction, the state change actions required that the voice recognizer understand a known action and a known device. When speaking scalar commands, the voice recognizer was required to interpret an additional command word (either "more" or "less"). It may be that these additional demands on the user and on the software, respectively, are responsible for the decreased success.

Table 8.1 Mean success rates across methods (m_v vs. m_g)

Task	p-value
t1: Turn on the light	0.486
t2: Turn off the light	0.346
t3: Turn on the a/c	0.585
t4: Turn on the radio	0.007*
t5: Turn off the radio	0.007*
t6: Open the blinds	0.450
t7: Close the blinds	1.000
t8: Open the blinds more	0.217
t9: Open the blinds less	0.597

Table 8.2 Mean success rates for m_v across order (m_v 1st vs. m_g 1st)

Task	p-value
t1: Turn on the light	0.542
t2: Turn off the light	0.121
t3: Turn on the a/c	1.000
t4: Turn on the radio	0.481
t5: Turn off the radio	0.154
t6: Open the blinds	1.000
t7: Close the blinds	1.000
t8: Open the blinds more	0.492
t9: Open the blinds less	0.705

Table 8.3 Mean success rates for m_g across order (m_v 1st vs. m_g 1st)

Task	p-value
t1: Turn on the light	0.295
t2: Turn off the light	0.279
t3: Turn on the a/c	0.431
t4: Turn on the radio	0.559
t5: Turn off the radio	0.559
t6: Open the blinds	0.066
t7: Close the blinds	1.000
t8: Open the blinds more	0.729
t9: Open the blinds less	0.721

Fig. 8.1 Mean success ratios according to interaction method

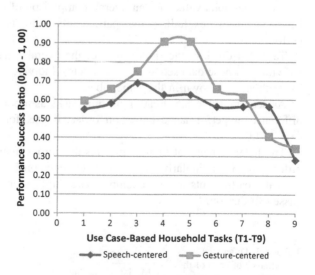

The variance between two sets of data can be compared using a Pearson's Chi-square test [1]. Applied to our general pools of performance data ($p <= 0.05$), this allowed us to test the hypothesis that there would be no significant difference in success rate when using either interactive method.

Table 8.4 Difference in performance of the two methods (m_v vs. m_g), in total and by task

Task	p-value
All Tasks	1.000
t1: Turn on the light	0.997
t2: Turn off the light	0.999
t3: Turn on the a/c	1.000
t4: Turn on the radio	1.000
t5: Turn off the radio	1.000
t6: Open the blinds	1.000
t7: Close the blinds	0.999
t8: Open the blinds more	0.999
t9: Open the blinds less	1.000

Like the t-Tests, the Chi-square test also showed no significant difference between voice-centered and gesture-centered interaction ($p = 1.000$). It may be worth noting here again that the data was not sufficiently robust to allow for a Chi-Square to be performed on all first attempts by all participants.

As mentioned above, one of our thirty-two participants failed to attempt the first and second tasks, and another failed to attempt the seventh task. This left us with three holes in our data table. These holes could be worked around in performing the overall Student's t-Tests, but not in performing overall or specific Pearson's Chi-Square tests [1]. Omitting the participants with the missing performances from the Pearson's Chi Square calculations enabled the generation of actual alpha values.

Thus, the alpha values for an overall comparison of the tasks by method had to be recalculated, excluding the participants who had missing data in their performances.

Table 8.4 displays the significance of the overall performance (minus the three individuals whose data sets were incomplete). Individual comparisons of each task, by method, are shown in the same table.

As seen in Table 8.5, treating all nine tasks as a pool, there was no significant difference in performance based on order of use, for either interactive method ($p = 1.000$).

The heterogeneity of first-attempt results across interaction type, regardless of order of use is particularly interesting when one considers that the protocol did not limit the participants to first attempts. The implications of all results will be discussed further on.

Table 8.5 Difference in performance of each of the two methods (m_v vs. m_g), by order

Order of performance	p-value
M_g 1st × M_g 2nd	1.000
M_v 1st × M_v 2nd	1.000

8.2 Second and Third Attempts: Measuring Intuitiveness

The data used to derive our quantitative results so far were based solely on first attempts at each command. This is a high standard for a prototypical device, especially for testing in which familiarization was not provided, or for testing in a noisy environment (as discussed previously).

That said, our intent was not to stop participants who did not succeed at first attempts, our intent was to see whether they could succeed within three immediately-consecutive attempts. That is, our intent was to see whether or not they could—without taking the time for conscious reflection and experimentation— intuit how to use the unfamiliar system to perform familiar tasks.

Participants had been directed to make no more than three failed attempts at each task before moving on to the next one. We set the limit at three immediately-successive failures based on the idea that more than three rapid attempts would require deliberate conscious processing or reflection, which is the antithesis of intuition [2].

The participants were significantly more successful when making one, two or three attempts than they were when only the first attempt is considered.

Success ratios for each task are grouped according to interaction method in Table 8.6, and it is clear that average performance of each task across participants improved given a second and third attempt. Analysis revealed that the overall

Table 8.6 Success at 1st attempt and by 3rd attempt

Method	Task	Success ratios	
		1st attempt	1st, 2nd, 3rd attempt
Voice-centered	T1: lights on	0.548	1.000
	T2: lights off	0.581	0.903
	T3: ac	0.688	0.938
	T4: radio on	0.625	0.969
	T5: radio off	0.625	0.906
	T6: blinds open	0.563	0.906
	T7: blinds closed	0.563	0.844
	T8: open more	0.563	0.719
	T9: open less	0.281	0.656
Gesture-centered	T1: lights on	0.594	0.938
	T2: lights off	0.656	0.938
	T3: ac	0.750	1.000
	T4: radio on	0.906	1.000
	T5: radio off	0.906	1.000
	T6: blinds open	0.656	0.938
	T7: blinds closed	0.613	0.871
	T8: open more	0.406	0.781
	T9: open less	0.344	0.781

Table 8.7 Success improved over the 1st 3 attempts

Comparing 1 attempt to 3	Alpha
t-Test of all tasks and methods	0.000
t-Test of all tasks m_v	0.000
t-Test of all tasks m_g	0.000

improvement was significant when success rates during first attempts are compared to success rates during first, second, and third attempts (as a group).

This comparison was made using a two-tailed within-group student's t-Test. The resultant alpha values, as shown in Table 8.7, reveal that the difference was statistically significant whether the performance was grouped according to method of interaction or generalized.

References

1. Claus G, Ebner H (1974) Grundlagen der Statistik für Psychologen. Pädagogen und Soziologen, Volk und Wissen
2. Zeigarnik B (1927) On the retention of completed and uncompleted activities. Psychologische Forschung 9:1–85

Chapter 9
"How Do You Feel?": Qualitative Results

Abstract The C.A.S.A. T.E.V.A. system was not designed solely to perform tasks with measurable success. The core intent was to design a new experimental means of interaction with a complex network of embedded devices that would not feel new, experimental, or complex. In this chapter we present the qualitative methods used to capture the feelings and opinions of the participants in our endeavor regarding the system. We used standard, pre- and post-experimental Likert questionnaires to gather consciously-expressed opinions, a System Usability Scale to turn some of those opinions into a deeper comparative evaluation of the system, and anthropological methods to gather unconscious opinions.

Keywords C.A.S.A. T.E.V.A. · HCI · Intuitive interaction · Multimodal interaction · Smart homes · Metrics · Gesture-based interaction · Voice-based interaction · Casa vecchia · Likert scale · System usability scale · Qualitative anthropological methods · Bellman's protocol · Triple modular redundancy · S.N.A.R.K. circuit

We report on three different methods of qualitative data collection. Likert scales were used to gather descriptive information regarding our participants and to survey their opinion of the techniques used in the experiment. The System Usability Scale (SUS) [1] was used to assess the usability of the system as a whole. Anthropological methods of observation and applied reasoning were used to assess performance and underlying meaning.

All thirty-nine of our original participants were surveyed before and after the experiment using standard Likert tests and the SUS. Furthermore, all were observed during the course of the experiment so that their performance and their behavior could be recorded. The data presented in this section reflects only the thirty-two participants who were, in the end, included in the quantitative data collection.

© The Author(s) 2017   55
J.N.A. Brown et al., *Building an Intuitive Multimodal Interface for a Smart Home*,
Human–Computer Interaction Series, DOI 10.1007/978-3-319-56532-3_9

9.1   Likert Scales: Perception of the System

Following the trial, each participant was asked a series of questions using a standard, five-choice Likert scale. There were sixteen questions presented. The first ten made up the SUS and will be discussed in Sect. 9.2. The eleventh question was a validation question, repeating a previous question to see if the participants were answering in a reliable fashion. All but one of the participants either repeated their previous answer or pointed out in writing that the question was a repeat. One participant was later removed from the pool because of difficulties with the English-language instructions.

The next five questions were a straightforward opinion survey regarding some of the features of the C.A.S.A. T.E.V.A. app. The questions and a summary of the answers are illustrated in Fig. 9.1.

Two participants, one male and one female, both speaking German as a first language, gave the lowest possible answer (Strongly disagree) to "I liked being able to name the system". All other responses ranged between 2 (Disagree) and 5 (Strongly agree). Mode and median scores for that statement were both 5 (Strongly agree). The same was true for "I would like to have a personalized smart computer system like this in my home or on my office" (range: 2–5). The three other statements all had responses ranging from 2 to 5, and all had mean and mode values of 4 (agree).

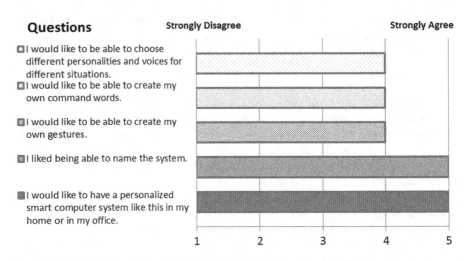

Fig. 9.1 Participants' opinion of C.A.S.A. T.E.V.A. features (mode values)

9.2 The System Usability Scale

Developed by Brooke, the System Usability Scale (SUS) is a 10-item Likert questionnaire with set questions and a simple means of normalization [1]. The original paper has been cited over 1700 times. Even-numbered questions have negative implications and odd numbered questions have positive implications. In order to have consistent scoring, the even-numbered scores are inverted (subtracted from five). Then the answers are normalized to a four-point scale and then multiplied by 2.5 for expression in a range of 0–100. This expression makes the SUS values look like percentages, but they are not. An SUS value of 50% does not mean an accuracy of 50%. It means that the person making the judgement perceives that the system being tested has a higher usability than 50% of all of the other systems that person uses as a mental comparison set when answering the questionnaire.

The participants rated perceived usability with a mean score of 77.03%, a median of 78.75% and a mode of 80%. The standard deviation was 10.15.

Based on these SUS scores (see Fig. 9.2), we can state that our participants, on average, felt that the usability of the C.A.S.A. T.E.V.A. application was higher than average.

9.3 Anthropological Methods and Our Conclusions

Likert scales are widely used, and the SUS has been used in over 500 studies since its inception. However popular these methods are in the field of computer science, the social sciences which depend upon qualitative data collection have largely

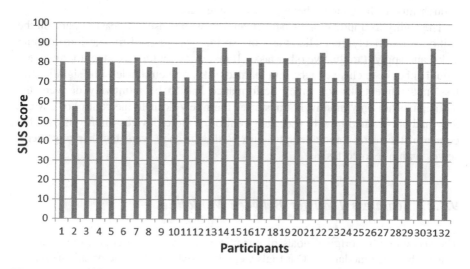

Fig. 9.2 Participant evaluation of C.A.S.A. T.E.V.A. usability, according to the SUS

turned to anthropological methods based on observation. This is because an opinion survey like a Likert scale can only collect the information that the user shares. Volunteered information is now considered to be inaccurate—whether consciously or unconsciously. In response to these concerns, we have introduced the use of anthropological methods in a few specific instances.

Anthropological methods of observation and deduction were specifically applied in order to judge true and false machine behavior during the trials, and to answer the three following issues: (1) the intuitive transition between devices; (2) the seamless transfer between modalities, both across and within methods, and; (3) the perception of the home as a single holistic entity.

9.3.1   Intuitive Transition Between Devices

The results presented immediately above show that, over the course of their first three attempts, the general pool of participants experienced significant improvement at all tasks. Please consider that, according to protocol, participants were not instructed in, or allowed to practice, the performance of every task. Participants were instead taught how to execute commands, but were only allowed to familiarize themselves with four tasks out of the nine.

In the case of m_g, the participants were each taught three gestural commands and were allowed to practice them on four tasks. In order to perform the five other tasks at all, each participant had to intuitively derive the relationship between the task they were asked to perform and the commands they had learned.

In the case of m_v, the participants were taught the syntax of the command structure and were given a task-order list which included the associated vocabulary. They were then encouraged to practice four of the nine tasks. They were not given enough time to familiarize themselves with the tasks.

The ability to improve one's performance must be based, at least in part, on the ability to intuitively generalize the tool use that was learned for the four training tasks, and apply it to the five other tasks. If this were not the case, the improvement would either be exclusive to the four learned tasks, or would at least be significantly less in the five tasks for which performance had to be intuitively derived. the participants not only intuitively transferred their new skills to the control of devices they had not learned how to use; their control of these devices improved over the course of their first three attempts—just as though they were familiarizing themselves with a learned task.

9.3.2   Seamless Transfer Between Modalities

The second of the original goals of our research is to try to support the seamless transfer between modalities. Our trials were designed based on the broad theoretical concepts presented in the first section of this book. The intent of the design has always been to force the computer to communicate in a more natural, more human manner. The result is multimodal communication designed to make use of the facts about natural human multimodality that have been discussed at length in Chap. 2.

While m_v is centered on voice, input is also generated via hand-clapping. While m_g is centered on the use of gestures, input also involves GUI button pushing and speech. In both cases, output is generated via speech, sound effect, GUI screen changes and two levels of written feedback, one of which provides a deeper feedback into the system's performance.

Given the multimodal nature of our interaction methods, "seamless transfer between modalities" could be taken to mean transferring between modalities while using a single interactional method, or when transferring from m_v to m_g (or vice versa).

9.3.3 Seamless Transfer Between Modalities Within Methods

In order to successfully perform a single task using either of the multimodal methods described above, a participant had to be able to transfer from one modality to another, synchronizing their own gestural and vocal signals and interpreting multimodal responses. Given mean performance ratios of 55.95% (m_v) or 64.84% (m_g), we must conclude that the seamless transfer between modalities that was required for successful interaction did in fact take place at least 55.95 and 64.84% of the time.

9.3.4 Seamless Transfer Between Modalities Across Methods

As was discussed in detail above the C.A.S.A. T.E.V.A. app worked on the basis of the illusion of a virtual major domo. This illusion is intended to provide relief from the need to work with multiple heterogeneous systems and the resultant techno-stress. The participants were meant to perceive a single holistic system with which they could interact using either of our two methods. While it was always understood that participants might develop an immediate preference for one interaction method over the other, the intent was to provide the future user with the option of choosing between two different methods of interacting with the same major domo, based on preference or on changing environmental conditions.

If the transfer from one method to the other was seamless, then we would expect no significant difference in performance between the two, regardless of the order in which they were used. As our results have shown there was no significant difference in overall general performance between methods in seven out of the nine tasks (Fig. 8.1). Order of use also showed no significant effect (Tables 8.2 and 8.3).

9.3.5 Perception of the Home as a Single Holistic Entity

The 32 participants who completed our study performed their nine tasks, once using our voice-centered methodology and once using our gesture-centered methodology. In each case they directed their command to the virtual major domo they had named. Every one of the users thanked the major domo at least once, calling it by name.

The participants were all working with a mental model that was centered upon the idea that the major domo—their personal invisible butler—would do the navigation for them. He would go from device to device, from control system to control system on their behalf in order to carry out their orders. They major domo navigated the ontology, but the participant did not have to.

Each participant performed their nine separate tasks, controlling four separate electronic devices in three separate locations, using a single mental model that carried over between interaction methodologies. Ipso facto, each participant was working with a mental model of their environment as a single, holistic entity.

Reference

1. Brooke J (1996) SUS: a "quick and dirty" usability scale. In: Jordan PW, Thomas B, Weerdmeester B, McClelland IL (eds) Usability evaluation in industry. Taylor & Francis, London, pp 189–194

Chapter 10
"...But Much yet Remains to Be Said": A Discussion of Our Failings and Success

Abstract As with all other experimentation, the formal testing of our S.N.A.R.K circuit was not conducted by flawless supermen who worked without error or setback. One of the joys of science is the sharing of our experimental limitations and the procedures that allowed us to cope with them. In this chapter, we share examples of the events that surprised us along the way: the unexpected obstacles, breakdowns, and intuitive leaps that made this journey all the more rewarding.

Keywords S.N.A.R.K. · Noise · Environmental interference · Calm technology · Ubiquitous computing · Intuitive interaction · King midas effect · Familiarization

Overall, our hunt for intuitive multimodal interaction was a success. As seen above, the research question was answered and the null hypotheses were disproven. That said, the study could have been better designed and better performed. Some aspects of the study reported are discussed here and conclusions are drawn.

10.1 Limitations

Like all original formal experiments, the current study faced a number of situations where a choice had to be made regarding how best to deal with an obstacle, whether that obstacle was anticipated or not. Hereunder, we report on two such obstacles and our attempts to mitigate their effect on our experiment. We recognize that four additional limitations of our study must be addressed in future studies.

© The Author(s) 2017   61
J.N.A. Brown et al., *Building an Intuitive Multimodal Interface for a Smart Home*,
Human–Computer Interaction Series, DOI 10.1007/978-3-319-56532-3_10

10.2   King Midas' Ring

A ring we had designed and built to be part of this system did not work in time to be included in our study. The "Wireless Or Not" (W.O.N.) Ring was designed to allow the user to gesture with an empty hand, and have those gestures recognized as though the smartphone were in use according to our gesture-centered protocol (m_g). The sensor purchased for this purpose was easily modified to fit on a ring and was successfully pilot tested as a gesture recognition device. Unfortunately, the device as purchased does not have an "off switch". This meant that all gestures were always being recognized and were always being used as a single, steady stream of input into our S.N.A.R.K. system. The researcher was faced with the choice of adding an additional set of trigger gestures, modifying the S.N.A.R.K., or delaying the testing. Time constraints outside of our control eliminated the possibility of delays. In the end, it was decided that it would be easier to modify the software to deal only with two input streams than it would be to develop, test and finalize a natural and universal trigger gesture that would not provide an additional cognitive load for the participant.

Modifications have been discussed and additional testing of the modified ring will begin soon. It is our intent to include the ring in future tests of the smart home system.

10.3   Background Noise

This was a deliberate factor; the normal, day-to-day noises of a shared office and laboratory space. We wanted to deal with realistic background noise levels and design our system such that these kind of noises would not have a negative impact either in terms of generating false positive signals or in terms of obscuring user attempts. That said, on a few occasions passerby generated noises or actions that were deliberately disruptive. On several occasions staff from the surrounding offices engaged in loud conversations on the balcony overlooking the lab space, or while walking through the experimental setting. One staff member elected to play a radio loudly whenever our experiment was going on.

One participant twice interrupted his protocol to enter into conversation with passerby. Given that this happened in only one of seventy-six trials—and then happened twice in succession—we elected to treat this as a conscious shift of focus on the part of the participant, and his data was removed from the pool.

The only other disruption caused by environmental conditions occurred when 6 passerby entered into a very loud discussion directly adjacent to a participant during her trial. During this conversation, first attempts at each task with m_v were all failures due to detection of their speech. The participant, showing signs of frustration, asked how she should proceed. She was encouraged to continue. In the end, she succeeded in performing five of the nine tasks successfully within three m_v

attempts. Despite growing success the participant expressed her frustration verbally and non-verbally (by failing to complete the tasks, by self-interruption in synch with the disruptive conversation, and by walking off-camera). The participant's m_g trial ran smoothly with results within the normal range (44.4% success—almost exactly one standard deviation from the mean). The damage had been done. With a missed task in her m_v trial, and visible effect of frustration on her performance, her data was excluded from the pool.

With these two exceptions, the experiment was not impeded by the noises in the environment and the results we have described were achieved despite these potentially-disruptive behaviors. This may be due to a combination of the perseverance of the majority of our participants, the degree to which the general population has become inured to environmental distractions while interacting with their smartphones, or the robustness of the system. These would all be interesting matters for future research.

These and other recommendations for future work will be provided in the final chapter, along with conclusions, discussions, and a summary of the contributions.

If Bardzell and Bardzell [1] were correct in their suggestion that Weiser's ideas of ubiquitous computing [2] and calm technology [3] have generated a bifurcated, rather than a holistic response; spurring engineers and technically-oriented scientists to pursue technological solutions, while driving psychologists and human-oriented scientists to pursue visionary new approaches, then this book is an attempt to build a bridge between the two groups.

Rather than pursuing a purely technological solution to the problem of unifying the interaction with distributed interfaces throughout a smart home, we have attempted to create interactive technology that works based on how humans naturally perceive, process, and respond to environmental stimuli. Key to this idea is the understanding that human perception is based on fitting incomplete information into recognized and anticipated patterns. Trying to completely fill a recognizable pattern often leads to an "uncanny valley" experience where unconscious perception of "false notes" shatters the illusion [4, 5]. As any worthy magician or psychologist would agree, the secret is to provide just enough information so that the subject subconsciously fills in the missing pieces and creates their own, richer illusion.

10.3.1 Reflections and Limitations

The work reported in this book has spanned three years, seven countries, and two continents. What had seemed at first to be the purely technical challenge of developing new hardware and software was revealed to be a problem lacking the fundamental theoretical groundwork that would underlie such work. In attempting to develop the practical, neurophysiological and anthropological underpinnings of Weiser's "Calm" [6], the solution to the original problem presented itself holistically; as a required combination of mental model and carefully-crafted illusion.

Interacting with the S.N.A.R.K. triggered the pre-attentive, pattern-recognizing processes in the minds of our participants to see a virtual butler trying to help them, even if he did not always succeed.

Unfortunately, some aspects of the S.N.A.R.K. were not executed as well as we would have liked. This hurt the illusion of helpfulness and reduced the quality of the experience.

10.4 The S.N.A.R.K. Was not Really a S.N.A.R.K.: Triple Redundancy

As discussed above, our protocol is based on the S.N.A.R.K. circuit: a triple redundancy input system based on command fail-safes developed for satellites more than a generation ago [7]. Triple redundancy should give three possible interpretations of each perceived signal:

(1) Three inputs of matching value are a clear signal of intent and the action should be carried out without further confirmation;
(2) Two inputs of matching value are an unclear signal of intent. Therefore, before any action is carried out, the system should output a request for confirmation of intent. At this point it is possible to ask for a single, double or triple follow-up input to serve as confirmation;
(3) When there are no inputs of matching value within the timeframe set for delineating the input series, all inputs should be treated as incomplete signals. In the normal course of events, the system continues to wait. If the system had already been triggered to expect a follow-up input—as in case (2), above—then it should either query to see if the expected follow-up is coming or alert the user to the fact that the allotted time interval has passed. This allows the user to easily rescind a failed attempt, simply by not following up.

Without the gesture-recognizing W.O.N. ring (as described above) the best case for input recognition could not occur. To put it simply, there was no way to give a perfect triply-redundant command. This means that our tests were conducted with a system that could only provide either failure or partial success. Given such a limitation, we are satisfied with our measured success ratios of 0.558 (m_v) and 0.649 (m_g).

10.5 Lack of Full Customization and Language Limitations

The intent of the Bellman's Protocol and the S.N.A.R.K. is to work with a totally user-derived lexicon, providing customized terminology for each activator and location in the house, as well as customized command words.

The underlying meaning of each term should be based on the use-case-derived command lexicon we have previously discussed, and the underlying meaning of each activator and location should be based on a state chart.

The viability of this totally personalized command system has been the subject of an as-yet unpublished study by Brown and Bouchachia using an Artificial Neural Network (ANN) to recognize a significant subset of the use-case derived commands and to recognize the voices of a variety of users [8]. This ANN was not available in the year leading up to the study we are now discussing, and so could not be included.

Additionally, it was decided not to ask each participant to decide on their own command words and names for each device to be tested. To do so would be a natural part of installing a smart home system, but we were concerned that it would bias our participants as regards their perception of the system as a single, holistic entity.

The immediate result was that the system we tested was deprived of an ANN that has a greater than ninety percent success rate at recognizing users and commands. In place of that near-perfect recognition, we used the publically-available, on-line English-language speech recognition engine by Google. Subsequently, the system we tested had some trouble coping with the accents of our multinational participants.

10.6 Unfamiliar Territory

Participants were shown how the device was used in both modalities. They were allowed to practice using the device, but they were not given time or opportunity to become familiar with the use of the entire command set. This was necessary so that we could measure whether or not they were able to intuitively interact with the system as a whole in a manner that seemed to them to be both holistic and logical, as per the original project description when it was initially conceived.

While this decision may have impacted negatively on our numbers, it also allowed us to draw a positive conclusion regarding the intuitiveness of the use of the system. Intuitive interaction and the perception of a logical and holistic smart home control system are discussed in the following chapter.

References

1. Bardzell J, Bardzell S (2013) A great and troubling beauty: cognitive speculation and ubiquitous computing. Personal Ubiquitous Comput 18(4):779–794
2. Weiser M (1993) Some computer science issues in ubiquitous computing. Commun ACM 36(7):75–84
3. Weiser M (1991) The computer for the twenty-first century. Sci Am 265(3):94–104
4. Mori M (1970) The uncanny valley. Energy 7(4):33–35

5. Geller T (2008) Overcoming the uncanny valley. IEEE Comput Graph Appl 28(4):11–17
6. Brown JNA (2016) Anthropology-based computing: putting the human in human-computer interaction. Springer Human Computer Interaction Series, Springer International Publishing, Switzerland
7. Kaschmitter JL, Shaeffer DL, Colella NJ, McKnett CL, Coakley PG (1991) Operation of commercial R3000 processors in the Low Earth Orbit (LEO) space environment. IEEE Trans Nucl Sci 38(6):1415–1420
8. Brown JNA, Bouchachia A (2012) AI-based recognition of multicultural users and of their use-case-based commands. Klagenfurt University, Austria (Unpublished report)

Chapter 11
"Yet, Still, Ever After...": Future Work

Abstract This book has been about the theoretical and practical work that went into developing a truly intuitive interface for controlling networked and embedded devices in the smart homes within and in parallel to the Casa Vecchia project. Both branches of that work continue, inside and outside of the Casa Vecchia system. In this final chapter we provide an overview of the theoretical and practical efforts that have derived from Casa Vecchia and from our work on the S.N.A.R.K.; and look into the future at what will come next.

Keywords Anthropology-based computing · Smart home · Casa Vecchia · C.A.S.A. T.E.V.A. · Automation · Augmented reality · Smart glasses · User experience · Wise home · Calm technology · B.O.O.J.U.M. · Bellman's protocol · S.N.A.R.K. · Intuitive interaction · B.R.A.I.N.S. · S.H.I.E.L.D.

11.1 "È un posto da Squili!"

The hunt for the S.N.A.R.K. is only one part of the Smart Home research that has been conducted in the context of the Casa Vecchia project. This final chapter aims to put a spotlight on the work that predated, ran in parallel to, and followed the main undertaking described in this book. The Casa Vecchia project, which has already been mentioned in the introductory chapter, was the foundation for the work we have presented in this book, and much more. Much of this was carried out in the many rural family homes that participated in the project over the years [1, 2], some was done in a particular sample home [3], and some—like the actual testing of the S.N.A.R.K.—was done in the somewhat artificial circumstances of the proverbial ivory tower of our university.

In these environments, experiments can be designed to avoid the confounding variables which are the almost unavoidable characteristics of the "real world". As a result, it is not surprising that most of the results developed and tested in artificial environments do not find their way into the hands of the real end user. There has not been enough hard research into precisely measuring the differences between

© The Author(s) 2017

J.N.A. Brown et al., *Building an Intuitive Multimodal Interface for a Smart Home*, Human–Computer Interaction Series, DOI 10.1007/978-3-319-56532-3_11

well-designed laboratory testing facilities and the average living environments they are meant to emulate. That there are differences is unquestioned. What is missing is a clear understanding of what, precisely, would make them more accurate.

This academic ignorance is especially true as one moves further from the lab geographically; moving for example, from the idea of individuals living in apartments, to the idea of the rural, multi-generational family home.

Casa Vecchia was trying to identify some of the barriers that might prevent the results of Smart Home research from being used by their purported target audience —elderly people living in their own rural family homes. To that end, we fitted their homes with state of the art smart home equipment for the duration of the project, and we interviewed, observed and accompanied those people as they became familiar with the new system in their home. We learned a lot. The first important thing was that new technology is more easily and fully accepted, as long as it is in the background. This, in a way, supports Venkatesh's approach emphasized in the introduction chapter (not the capability of technology is important, but its match to human wants) [4].

"Smartness" means that the enhanced functions would have to work automatically, without disturbing the familiar behaviours, activities and routines that take place in a household. This is specifically important in the context of safety and security. If something dangerous happened, it would not make sense to actively press a button, even if it were the kind of wrist-band emergency button that is frequently used by nursing organizations. Things that have to be carried as an additional device seem to carry the psychological barrier of being dependent, being stigmatized by having to carry the red button on the wrist. So real world seniors tend to avoid these devices [5].

Really "smart" technology should work in the background, triggering automatically, on the basis of personal and environmental sensors. In this regard two colleagues have to be mentioned for their work in the domains of activity recognition and deviation identification [6, 7]. Their work further advanced the platform described in detail throughout this book, and the enhancements that grew out of their efforts was another important step in the further development of the system.

Unfortunately, the Casa Vecchia programme ended before we could fully implement the "Calm" technology of the S.N.A.R.K. in the rural homes that were our major testbed. The participants in the Casa Vecchia project should have had the chance, not only to benefit from security features, but also to actively control their environment, communicate with other people and search for information. However, the pre-S.N.A.R.K. models and concepts of Smart Home interaction turned out to be largely inappropriate for "real world" seniors.

As an illustrative example, consider the idea that one should carry a Smart Home interface device that would work like the remote control of a television. For several reasons (e.g. decreasing memory capabilities) elderly people tend to have a routine of keeping common tools and devices in specific places, so as to more easily find them when needed. This means that the device is not at hand, but sitting in a location selected for easy remembering. If the device is not at hand, then it cannot be used spontaneously. To put it another way, sometimes remote controls are, as the name could imply, not only remote from the device, but also from the user.

Because of things such as electric smog [8], the elderly also do not tend to keep their smartphone with them at all times. Because of concerns about energy consumption based on the technological conditions of a previous generation, the elderly tend to switch off their phones when they are not using them. The predominant assumption that the smartphone is "always on" changes for most of the elderly to an assumption that the device is "always off"—a condition that impedes much of the "obvious" and "commonplace" use of a smartphone among the general population.

There is another important factor which impedes the use of some aspects of modern technology, among the elderly and other groups as well: the complexity of the interfaces.

The elderly or, at least, most of the current cohort of the elderly, are not familiar with complex touchscreen interfaces, and are not willing or even able to learn to interact with them. Consider, they come from a time when one didn't toggle switches to see what worked for fear of breaking something. This is in stark contrast to today's software users.

If it had been possible to implement the S.N.A.R.K. into the households of the elderly in our Casa Vecchia project, this would have fulfilled many of the needs that we derived from our work with them. The technology would have settled, unseen, into the background and would not have disturbed the familiar activities taking place in the home. Basing interaction with the smart component on natural patterns of interaction known from human to human interaction—the natural combination of intuitive gesture and speech—might have echoed Clarke's Third Law,[1] seeming to avoid technology entirely, and resorting, instead, to magic.

11.2 "The Moment One Looked in His Face"

The findings of Casa Vecchia and our other activities in the domain of smart environments all led to the same assumption—that state of the art smartness is not enough, because it is not really smart. In the best case, today's "smart devices" are simply dumb. In the worst cases, they seem actually to be more "smart ass".

This led to the idea of reconsidering the whole concept in an attempt to bring it to another level. This meant more than just trying to enhance or improve the existing concept; it meant trying to go beyond it.

Some examples in history inspired the idea. The grandson of Henry Ford has often remarked on his grandfather's intuitive leap from the horse-drawn carriage to

---

[1]"Any sufficiently advanced technology is indistinguishable from magic." From Clarke A.C. (1962, rev. 1973). "Hazards of Prophecy: The Failure of Imagination" in the collection Profiles of the Future: An Enquiry into the Limits of the Possible, p. 36.

the "horseless carriage". If the older Ford, it is implied, had only observed current developments, market demand and consumer needs, he would have focused on trying to provide his customers with "a faster horse".

For a more recent example, please consider the ipod. When it was introduced, the market was characterized by media players based on portable and changeable media, compact cassettes, compact disks, mini discs, and so on. These examples were just an enhancement of existing technology (a better compact cassette): one might say they were examples of thinking inside, rather than outside, of the box. This way of thinking is still both common and popular. Consider the inherent message in phrases like "Web 2.0", "Industry 4.0", and so on.

Coming back to the smart environments, the intent built from our reconsideration of what it means to be smart was not to introduce a Smart Home 2.0. Instead, the concept's name should clearly reflect a paradigmatic change in what should be expected from the next generation of "smart" technology.

In human cognitive development, the next stage after "intelligence" or "smartness" is the development of "wisdom". Thus, the next stage in the development of a house full of functional "smart" technology would reflect the next step in cognition. The label of the new concept was "The Wise Home" [9].

The wise home concept was one theoretical outcome of the research environment that surrounded our hunt for the S.N.A.R.K. The hunt revealed many shortcomings and drawbacks of current smart technology, within our work and in the literature. It became clear that current technology was not appropriately meeting the interactional needs of its users. In many cases, common attempts at recommender systems and other assistive technologies and devices even gave the impression of trying to take control away from the user entirely.

One can observe similar patterns of behaviour in people who might be described as "smart". To paraphrase Sternberg, smart people are more susceptible to certain fallacies in their thinking; cognitive fallacies such as egocentrism and feelings of omniscience or even omnipotence [10]. These same attitudes were being conveyed during the use of a state of the art smart system—not by the human, but by the machines.

For example, consider what might follow the following spoken command, if your state of the current art Smart Home were speech-enabled: "Smart home, I want to change the temperature". If a state of the art home were able to speak in a manner that reflected it's actual programming, it might say "Based on my infallible algorithms, the current temperature is optimal in terms of both comfort and energy consumption. Your subjective impression of temperature is an irrelevant outlier in my vast databases".

That might seem silly, but smart homes currently convey that same message—they just do so in a more subtle manner, by preventing you from changing the settings. That might be accomplished with inherent complexity, or with direct password protection.

Consider, in contrast, how a wise person might respond to a similar request. For our example, let us use the prototype of a wise and charismatic person, a grandmother playing with her grandchild. Of course the grandmother has way more experience, smartness, knowledge, and wisdom than the child, but would she simply shut the child out of the decision-making process? Wouldn't she find a way to recognize and value the child's concerns and desires, all while providing the opportunity to evaluate the situation with added information mitigated by kindness and respect.

Let's take the grandmother out of the home and into a playground, so consider another illustration. At the park, the small child wants to ride the swings, something he cannot do safely. Would a wise grandmother simply refuse? Would she prevent the child from using the swings, or would she use the opportunity for something more. A smart home might cite statistics about accidents, or simply fall back on a restriction based on the fact that the child has never used the swings before. But a wise grandmother might say: "Let's use the swings together. I'll help you climb up, and I'll give you a little push to get you going. If you need help, I'm right here." She would say this all in a way that the child could understand, and she would repeat or rephrase the offer of help if changing conditions made it likely to be seen as considerate, rather than controlling. Of course, a wise grandmother would keep her hands on or near the child, and would use each little push to help maintain the child's balance so that the experience would be more likely to be successful and pleasant. The child would never know just how much of his pleasant success was due to his grandmother's assistance, and that would be just fine.

This is what we would wish for the home of the future, wisdom based on a seamless benevolent cooperation between humans and the computerized systems that assist them in being pleasantly successful.

11.3 "And Seemed Almost Too Good to Be True"

One branch of our ongoing research addresses the application of Augmented Reality (AR) within the Smart Home context in order to support comprehension and maintenance of complex automated systems.

Smart Home technology will further evolve and new devices, services and means to interconnect them will become available and provide new opportunities to extend existing installations. Individual household structures, residents and their needs and habits will also change over time. Designers of automated systems may not be able to fully incorporate such future changes in advance which results in an ongoing (lifelong) process of optimization and adaption of Smart Home technology. It would be sensible to give residents the chance to contribute to the technical setup and configuration on their own, not only for economic reasons (cost for service personnel) but especially to achieve ideal adaption to individual needs. Especially when incorrect automated functions interfere with elementary needs (nutrition, heating, security) accessible possibilities for immediate interventions are crucial.

It is not only laypersons who may easily be overburdened by complex interconnected systems. In contrast to building automation in the public and industrial sector Smart Home solutions are less based on common standards which e.g. is especially true for the various wireless Smart Home systems that can be used to retrofit existing (older) buildings. In combination with other systems in a home (e.g. internet connections, local networks, multimedia devices) challenges arising from complexity also grow for professional service personnel (e.g. the local electrician) [9].

If one is trying to implement Weiser's "Calm technology", as discussed at length in earlier chapters then residents should not be bothered with technical details regarding their homes. Augmented Reality (AR) is able to enrich our view on the real world with computer-generated content as an additional information source that can be accessed on demand. In the Smart Home context such information may contain states, rules and functions of the underlying automation systems. This could help users to build up adequate individual mental models of complex installations and guide them in necessary maintenance and adaption steps.

Figure 11.1 illustrates a possible scenario: A wireless motion sensor controls the lights in the hallway and the kitchen e.g. to realize a light corridor for safety reasons. If the light corridor stops working for some reason a user (a layperson or expert) may start an AR application on a tablet or smartglass. By scanning a marker on the sensor the application provides additional information out of the Smart Home automation system running in the background. In our scenario the battery is empty and has to be changed. In a next step the AR view may show instructions where the battery is located and how it is changed.

However, when attempting to use one piece of technology in order to tame another, one must be very careful so as not to actually increase the overall problem. Selection and evaluation of the ideal hardware platform (e.g. hand-held vs.

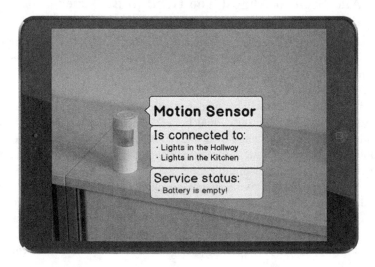

Fig. 11.1 Illustrates a possible AR—based scenario

head-worn devices) as well as their combination with different input and output modalities (speech, gesture, gaze, etc.) to support AR based solution within the Smart Home are therefore topics of our ongoing research.

11.4 "...Bellowing on to the Last"

On a purely practical level, the concepts of the S.N.A.R.K. and B.O.O.J.U.M. (Chap. 4) should be applied and tested independently, by other teams, using standard methods, to see if they do function as well as we have observed. We ourselves plan to test a next generation of S.N.A.R.K. and B.O.O.J.U.M., part and parcel with a new generation of the C.A.S.A. T.E.V.A. app and a W.O.N. ring (Chap. 4). But the development of practical, useful, accurate tools is only one aspect of the development of a good user experience. The technology must be based on an understanding of how we, as humans, might think about using it.

The need for a formal theory of how humans interact with their environment led to the development of "Anthropology-Based Computing" (ABC). As explained in the eponymous book, ABC "is the application of the fundamentals of Anthropology in order to remake traditional Human-Computer Interaction into a science that is truly based on humans, instead of the motley series of brilliant innovations, glorified mistakes, and obscure Cross-Generational Habits that comprise the computer-centered HCI that we practice today" [11].

To further quote from that book: "The goals of ABC are to explain why Weiser was right to say that HCI must be changed when computers become ubiquitous, and to show how that might be done." In order to accomplish this, Weiser's concept of "Calm" had to be explained in quantitative terms. This led to the development of the ABC model of Calm Interaction [13], which is based on the fairly-obvious but largely-ignored idea that humans do not interact with the world around them in a purely thoughtful manner. A simple summary was provided in the final chapter of the book Application of Big Data for National Security [14].

> This is in contrast to previous models of HCI, which illustrated human perception, processing, and reaction as happening in a single cycle. The single-cycle models fail to account for the natural human ability to interact with peripheral information, dealing with some stimuli either reflexively or pre-attentively, while simultaneously dealing with separate stimuli in a cognitive or attentive manner.

The ABC model of HCI is a formal model of how the long-discussed triune nature of the human brain might really work. This is the notion that reflexes, reactions, and reasoning all happen in different parts of the brain, reflecting the evolution of the physiological structures of what McClain famously called "The Lizard Brain", "The Paleo-Mammalian Brain", and "The Neo-Mammalian Brain" [11].

The new, ABC-based model updates the locations and functions of the three sections from McClain's triune model, and their relative evolutionary ages as well.

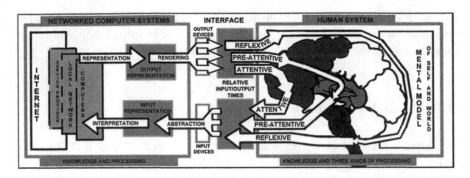

Fig. 11.2 The modes of interaction are illustrated in a traditional tennis court-style model

The modes of interaction are illustrated in a traditional tennis court-style model, with the human and computer facing each other across a barrier intended to represent the interface between them (Fig. 11.2).

Like other models of interaction, the ABC model of HCI can seem off-putting due to its complexity. As shown in Fig. 11.3, the evolutionary and functional structure of the triune brain is illustrated in more clearly and intuitively in a model called Brown's Representation of Anthropogenic Interaction in Natural Settings (B. R.A.I.N.S.) [11].

Following the path set upon in the hunt for the S.N.A.R.K., B.R.A.I.N.S. is another amusingly-named, but seriously intended attempt to advance our understanding of the way we work with computerized systems, not only among experts in HCI, but for everyone who uses computers and computerized tools.

Fig. 11.3 The BRAINS model of the triune nature of the human brain, as reflected in all human-centered interaction

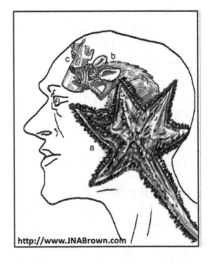

Such a widespread dissemination is necessary. These tools are everywhere, and their effects are—for the most part—going unmeasured.

No one expected that the widespread dissemination of electronic mail systems would lead to incessant interruption or that text messaging functions on portable phones would mean that we would be in constant low-fidelity communication throughout the waking day. How will incessant communication expand when every wall, window and door of our homes is automated? How will our 'time to be more fully human' diminish when every device in and around our lives is always on the verge of demanding that we stop everything and reply to the technological equivalent of a newborn baby's inchoate and inarticulate demands for attention? [11]

The theoretical insights and real-world demands described above combined to advance the development of the ABC model of interaction, and the invention of several means of applying it.

In 2014, the World Health Organization (WHO) announced that driving while distracted by a smartphone had become the leading cause of death of people aged 15–29. If you fall within that age group, you are four times more likely to be involved in a fatal crash while using a phone than if you are driving without one [11]. We turned to the BRAINS model to attempt to develop a non-distracting alert system. Would it be possible to develop an alert that could inform the intended recipient without interrupting their work or disturbing others? The answer seemed to be yes [11].

The original concept for the S.N.A.R.K. circuit was inspired by a decades-old solution to the problem of accurate satellite communications. The concept for ABC-based alerts was inspired by an even older concept from the field of cognitive psychology. The cocktail party effect describes how humans can be observed to focus their attention on selected streams of input while successfully ignoring parallel streams that are every bit as robust; listening to one stream of conversation while ignoring all of the others conversations of a crowded room [12].

Further studies had shown that some noises break through the internal mechanism that keeps us from understanding the conversations we are ignoring, based on emotional value. You will hear your name when it is spoken, even across a crowded and noisy room, and the same seems to be true of any word spoken by someone to whom you have a strong emotional attachment [15]. There had even been more recent studies purporting to have detected activity in different parts of the brain based on whether a conversation was being consciously attended or subconsciously ignored.

To study this further, the ABC research group expanded from the living lab in southern Austria into a Psychology lab in southern Portugal.

There, a complex study was designed to measure whether not these alerts could work. The results were very promising [15]. At the time of this writing, follow-up trials are underway back at the Living Lab in Austria. Both teams are also developing a testing protocol for a "Calm" replacement for pop-up messages based on the same principal.

Finally, we are trying to further develop two previously published ideas that stem from the B.R.A.I.N.S. model. The first is a matrix for simply evaluating whether a given task exceeds our reflexive, reactive, and/or reflective capabilities.

Classification of Attenional demands in a Layered Matrix			
ELEMENTS	**DEMANDS**		
	REFLEXIVE	PRE-ATTENTIVE	ATTENTIVE
START			
FLOW			
PAUSE			
RESUME			
STOP			
WORST CASE			

Fig. 11.4 CALMatrix for overlapping tasks

We call it the "Classification of Attentional Demands in a Layered Matrix" (CALMatrix) (Fig. 11.4).

Once any given task has been evaluated in this way, its matrix can be layered with other matrices showing the demands of other tasks, thus allowing a quick and easy insight into whether or not it might exceed our capabilities to try and perform these two tasks at once. The same concept can be extended to evaluating the demands on alerts and alarms, to see how the interface can make it dangerous to deal with a particular alarm or alert during the performance of common tasks (Fig. 11.5).

These two types of matrices could become a useful tool for teaching why practice can make it safe to walk while juggling, but nothing can make it safe to interact with a dashboard navigational device while driving.

The same principal of layered matrices has been applied to the field of Hazard recognition and mitigation with the development of a system for "Simple Hazard Identification through the Evaluation of Layered Displays" (S.H.I.E.L.D.). As illustrated in Fig. 11.6, SHIELD supports the identification of concurrent known hazards in situations where one or more people perform simultaneous, overlapping

CALMatrix for Signals and Alarms			
RESPONSES	**DEMANDS**		
	REFLEXIVE	PRE-ATTENTIVE	ATTENTIVE
PERCEIVE			
PROCESS			
DELAY (snooze)			
DENY			
ACCEPT			
IGNORE			

Fig. 11.5 CALMatrix for alarms and alerts

Simple Hazard Identification through the Evaluation of Layered Displays		
INTERRUPTIVE EVENT	Possible? Y/N	REMEDIAL ACTIONS (PRE- & POST-)
MINOR DISTRACTION		
MAJOR DISTRACTION		
PHYSICAL BREAK		
MENTAL BREAK		
TOOL FAILURE		

Fig. 11.6 SHIELD, a matrix for the identification and mitigation of hazards

tasks. An expert can then layout a mitigation plan for each level of hazard, and see whether their strategies would interfere with one another. This could be a useful tool for common hazardous tasks such as piloting a plane, driving a car, or walking and talking at the same time [16].

11.5   "It Is Ages Ahead of the Fashion"

In their deeply reflective 2013 examination of the cognitive speculation underlying Weiser's conjoined visions of ubiquitous computing and calm technology, Bardzell and Bardzell [17] explain the rift in the work that has been done since. They posit that the technical work that could be done towards computational ubiquity was easily-envisaged and pursued, and that it has been updated in accordance with advances in the field. On the other hand, the visionary, human-centered aspects that should be based in psychology and anthropology have been set aside. They call for Weiser's vision to be updated "in a cognitive, rather than fantasy-based way". They offer hopeful guidelines for the updated vision:

> Steeped in a substantial mastery of ubicomp's empirical present (as Weiser was in his time), an updated vision will critically reimagine human experience in light of a present expert understanding of what a ubiquitous computing environment could be. This new vision will incorporate a holistic picture of what ubiquitous computing might look like, and it will relate it to an understanding of how human subjectivity itself might persist and change in this new reality, rendering visible previously hidden potential pitfalls and benefits alike. Such an understanding should destabilize present received assumptions about the "the user" and reopen the conceptualization of the user itself to both critical interrogation and empirical evaluation [17].

The principal work in this book has been nothing more or less than an attempt to update Weiser's vision of "Calm" in a practicable manner. We have attempted to deal with both the visionary and technical sides of "Calm" and so to heal the rift in the original work that has been growing for the last two decades.

We have undertaken this healing from both sides of the wound, by giving the vision a rigorous scientific foundation in human cognition, and by giving the technical side working examples of an interface that uses holistic and human-centered mental models to create a user experience that seems, measurably, to be intuitive and easy.

References

1. Leitner G, Fercher A (2010) AAL 4 ALL—a matter of user experience. Aging Friendly Technology for Health and Independence, pp 195–202
2. Leitner G, Fercher A, Felfernig A, Hitz M (2012) Reducing the entry threshold of AAL systems: preliminary results from casa vecchia. In: Miesenberger K, Karshmer A, Penaz P, Zagler W (eds) Computers helping people with special needs, vol 7382, 1st edn., Lecture notes in computer scienceSpringer, Heidelberg, pp 709–715
3. Ayuningtyas CH, Leitner G, Funk M, Hu J, Hitz M, Rauterberg M (2014) Activity monitoring for multi-inhabitant smart homes. SPIE Newsroom, Den Haag
4. Venkatesh A (1996) Computers and other interactive technologies for the home. Commun ACM 39(12):47–54
5. Hirsch T, Forlizzi J, Hyder E, Goetz J, Kurtz C, Stroback J (2000) The ELDer project: social, emotional, and environmental factors in the design of eldercare technologies. In: Proceedings on the 2000 conference on universal usability. ACM, pp 72–79
6. Samselnig R (2012) Ein Smarthome lernt Ortsabhängigkeit. Diploma Thesis, Alpen-Adria Universität Klagenfurt, Klagenfurt
7. Grötschnig B (2011) Erkennung von Verhaltensmustern in Smart Homes zur Unterstützung älterer Menschen. Diploma Thesis, Alpen-Adria Universität Klagenfurt, Klagenfurt
8. Leitner G, Felfernig A, Fercher AJ, Hitz M (2014) Disseminating ambient assisted living in rural areas. Sens Spec Issue Ambient Assist Living 14(8):13496–13531
9. Leitner G (2015) The future home is wise, not smart. Springer, London
10. Sternberg RJ (2004) What is wisdom and how can we develop it? Ann Am Acad Polit Soc Sci 591(1):164–174
11. Brown JNA (2015) Anthropology-based computing. Springer, Cham, Switzerland
12. Conway AR, Cowan N, Bunting MF (2001) The cocktail party phenomenon revisited: the importance of working memory capacity. Psychon Bull Rev 8(2):331–335
13. Brown JNA, Leitner G, Hitz M, Català Mallofré A (2014) A model of calm HCI. In: Bakker S, Hausen D, Selker T, van den Hoven E, Butz A, Eggen B (eds) Peripheral interaction: shaping the research and design space. Workshop at CHI2014, Toronto, Canada. ISSN: 1862-5207
14. Brown JNA (2015) Making sense of the noise: an ABC approach to big data and security. In: Akhgar B, Saathoff GB, Arabnia HR, Hill R, Staniforth A, Bayerl PS (eds) Application of big data for national security: a practitioner's guide to emerging technologies. Butterworth-Heinemann
15. Brown JNA, Oliveira J, Bakker S (2015) I am calm: towards a psychoneurological evaluation of ABC ringtones. Interact Des Archit 26:55–69
16. Brown JNA, Bayerl PS, Fercher A, Leitner G, Català Mallofré A, Hitz M (2014) A measure of calm. In: Bakker S, Hausen D, Selker T, van den Hoven E, Butz A, Eggen B (eds) Peripheral interaction: shaping the research and design space. Workshop at CHI2014, Toronto, Canada. ISSN: 1862-5207
17. Bardzell J, Bardzell S (2013) "A great and troubling beauty": cognitive speculation and ubiquitous computing. Pers Ubiquitous Comput 1–16

Printed in the United States
By Bookmasters